"We are the stewards of this special place. It is up to us to keep it from slipping through our fingers."
--Terrell Lester, Artist
"Heart Island Sunset"
(cover photo)

DELICIOUS DEER ISLE

Celebrating the 100th Anniversary of Sunset Congregational Church
Sunset, Maine

We dedicate Delicious Deer Isle to our former Pastor and friend, the Reverend Alice A. Hildebrand, who shepherded the Sunset Church congregation in a loving and caring way for seven years. She ministered to our families for christenings, weddings, and memorial services. She was with us in times of happiness and in times of sadness. She listened to us. She led us. She gave us hope. We truly are grateful to her for the many gifts that she gave us, and we will draw on her guidance as we approach the next 100 years.

Published in 2012 by

Deer Isle Sunset Congregational Church
Deer Isle and Sunset, Maine

Printed in the United States of America

First Edition

Second Printing

Copyright © Deer Isle Sunset Congregational Church 2012

All rights reserved. No part of this book may be reproduced in any form, without written permission, except by a newspaper or magazine reviewer who wishes to quote brief passages in connection with a review.

A Message To Our Readers

Delicious Deer Isle celebrates the 100th anniversary of the Sunset Congregational Church of Deer Isle, Maine. It brings together the variety of tastes, textures, and treasures of our community, highlighting and validating our uniqueness. Sunset Congregational Church is a small church that plays a central stabilizing role in the community of the island. Its mission states:

> *"We are an historic congregation of the United Church of Christ (UCC) with deep roots in the New England Congregational Church. We are a community church, dedicated to serving the needs of our diverse population. Our island setting means that we are closely knit to one another; our heritage is to be engaged with the wider world. We believe that God is still speaking; that God is doing new things in our midst; and that faith, hope, and love will have the last word."*

The recipes in this book have been collected and collated lovingly over the past year. They reflect the diverse interests of the island population, which is composed of full-time residents and seasonal residents whose families have been summering here for over 130 years. This book has grown out of a love for God, a love for the church, a love for the island, a love for each other, and a love of food. It is our hope that, through this book, the reader will learn to love Deer Isle as much as we do.

We express deep appreciation to those who have made the publication of this book a reality: Paul Loggins of Backstage Entertainment, Nashville, TN provided editing and design. Marnie Reed Crowell and Ann Flewelling, who work together as Threehalf Press, gave us guidance and front and back cover design. Our thanks to Interim Minister, Rev. Dana Douglass, for his assistance with the scripture selections. Lucy Vander Mel guided us as a member of the Centennial Committee. Terrell Lester provided the front cover photograph and Stephanie Bartron-Miscione provided the back cover original painting. Tim Vander Mel contributed creative poetry and drawings for our chapter headings. Suzanne Decrow's help was very valuable and we thank her for her guidance. Many church members, family members and friends contributed the delicious, delectable, and delightful recipes. We hope that this book brings you great enjoyment through reading, cooking, and savoring the moment.

The committee would like to thank the many others whose names are not mentioned who have supported this project during the publishing phase. Every effort to avoid error has been made. We ask your forgiveness if errors are found.

Faithfully,

The Cookbook Committee (also known as "The Cookies")

Elana Anderson
Carol Bischoff
Barbara L. H. Chesney
Charlotte Davis
Anette Jaquette
Marydel Rosenfield
Eliza Spencer

"So whether you eat or drink, or whatever you do, do all to the glory of God."

1 Corinthians 10:31

Table of Contents

A Message To Our Readers 5

Church History 8

Chapter 1: **SALADS** 15

Chapter 2: **APPETIZERS** 35

Chapter 3: **SOUPS** 51

Chapter 4: **BEVERAGES** 59

Chapter 5: **BREADS & ROLLS** 69

Chapter 6: **COOKIES & BARS** 81

Chapter 7: **DESSERTS** 97

Chapter 8: **MAIN DISHES** 129

Chapter 9: **VEGETABLES & SIDE DISHES** 149

Chapter 10: **SEAFOOD** 163

Chapter 11: **BREAKFAST & BRUNCH** 179

Chapter 12: **THIS & THAT** 189

Chapter 13: **CELEBRATIONS** 207

References 217

Index 219

Sunset Congregational Church — Sunset, Maine

HISTORY OF SUNSET CONGREGATIONAL CHURCH
Barbara L.H. Chesney

Little is known about the earliest beginnings of Sunset Congregational Church. It grew from prayer groups that met in homes in the Sunset area of Deer Isle, Maine. It evolved to meet the needs of the community, and it therefore became a reflection of the community.

The first permanent settlement was made in Deer Isle in 1762, the first frame house was built in 1771, and the Town of Deer Isle was incorporated in 1789. Some of the early settlers came to the island on two-masted schooners that were tied to the dock at Northwest Harbor at high tide so that they would remain upright when the tide went out. When the tide came in, the boats were untied, and they sailed to other ports.

At one time, Deer Isle Village had more than 50 businesses, including a blacksmith shop, a meat market, a dry goods store, a jewelry store, a doctor, a dentist, and an ice cream shop. The major commercial interests were shipbuilding, shipping, sail making, ice cutting, bay coasting and carrying freight, and the making of pants. In the mid-1800s, summer visitors and tourists came to the island. Inns and small hotels developed. Yachting became an occupation as hundreds of island men were hired as captains, mates, and crew. In the home, women made candles, soap and spun wool and flax. Outside, women worked in seafood factories canning crab, lobster, and sardines. Farmers raised rye, corn, and wheat. Lumber was milled. Bricks were made in brickyards, and silver, asbestos, and copper were mined. Marble and granite

Main St., Deer Isle, Me.

were quarried. Salt and rum were imported.

With the shipping industry that developed and with ships arriving from afar, rum was plentiful on Deer Isle and sold for 16 cents a pint. The women of the island reacted to the lifestyle of intemperance that their husbands were acquiring, and in 1835 a group of women who lived in the area of the island known as "Sunset" decided to seek solace in companionship. They began meeting in homes to discuss the evils of drinking and to support a national movement known as the Washingtonian Movement, whose goal was to prohibit the use of alcohol.

This group of women became known as the Martha Washington Temperance Society, and with time, they decided to benefit their community in addition to eradicating intemperance. The "Weekly Packet," published in Blue Hill, Maine, reported that the "Marthas" had one project of sewing and distributing clothing for the destitute, especially those who had reached this state as a result of excessive use of liquor. Being an active group, the Martha Washington Temperance Society of Sunset sent their youngest members to collect wool from all those who kept sheep. They "picked," carded, and spun the wool and knitted socks that sold for 30 -35 cents a pair. Annually, they held a Spinning Bee. All spinning wheels, swifts, and reels of the neighborhood were brought to a meeting place, and a dinner was held with baked beans, brown bread, Indian pudding, and various cakes and pies. Every woman in the community belonged to the Martha Washington Benevolent Society, and a camaraderie that was based on an understanding of "union and harmony" developed among them.

In 1843, the group changed its name to the Martha Washington Benevolent Society and changed its place of meeting to the Sunset Schoolhouse, located on the land that is now known as the Village Green. When the schoolhouse burned, the "Marthas" arranged with the school district to pay for the second floor of the new schoolhouse. This floor was called "Monitor Hall," and served to hold community meetings as well as the meetings of the Martha Washington Benevolent Society. Today the Schoolhouse and the Monitor Hall do not exist. Instead, the Village Green, a beautiful fenced garden, occupies the land on the corner adjacent to Sunset Congregational Church. Community events, such as receptions for christenings and the Blessing of The Pets occur there today.

When the Old Burying Ground in Deer Isle became crowded, making it impossible for the segregation of families, and when

HISTORY

Sunset Chapel 1899

the "Marthas" felt that they needed their own cemetery, they found a spot on a farm. They convinced the owner to make it available, and the women formed a corporation so that they could own the Hillside Cemetery property. The land was partitioned into lots that were sold to help pay for the land, and improvements were begun. In 1864, the President of the Martha Washington Benevolent Society died, and she became the first to be laid to rest in Hillside Cemetery. Other charter members of the organization were buried there later.

The early congregation of Sunset Congregational Church evolved from a prayer group that met in the homes of members and in the Monitor Hall above the Schoolhouse. In 1879, land was purchased for South West Chapel, later known as Sunset Church. In 1884, South West Chapel was complete. Improvements were made over the years, such as covering the original plaster walls with decorative steel paneling. Pews were installed, the wood-fired stove was replaced with gas furnaces, and electric light fixtures replaced kerosene lamps.

When South West Chapel was constructed, the Martha Washington Benevolent Society offered to help financially so that they could use the Balcony of the chapel to hold their meetings. They met there for many years and decorated it, using a circular ceiling design around a chandelier and wall inscriptions of a logo with the date 1835 and a statement of their motto: "Whatsoever Thy Hand Find To Do. Do it With Thy Might." All three were painted in yellow tan, rosy beige, and light gray.

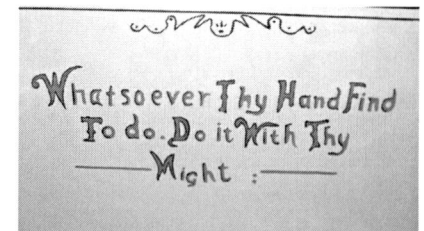

In 1899, two dollars was donated to the Martha Washington Society. The Society used the money to purchase a large lamp to be placed outside the Chapel near the entrance. In 1900, they voted to recall a previous vote to build a sidewalk and then voted unanimously to build a Hall that would contain a library and reading room. In 1902, this Hall was constructed with $800.00 that the "Marthas" had raised. It was used for lectures, concerts, fairs, and other forms of entertainment and social events. Dancing, however, was not allowed in the Hall.

By 1943, the Martha Washington Benevolent Society became inactive. The Society deeded the Hall, known as the Library and then as the Parish House, to Sunset Congregational Church. The Parish House was enlarged and modified in 1957.

In 1912, the Chapel Association merged with other groups that developed after 1884. The Society of Christian-Workers was formed in 1892, and the 1900's Student Ministers was formed. These groups along with the Chapel Association became Sunset Congregational Church.

The church organization had a President, Vice President, Treasurer, and Secretary. It had a Constitution written from Covenants used by a Bar Harbor church and by a Stonington church. It organized with 14 charter members on May 10, 1912, with the Conference Minister and the Maine Sea Coast Mission in attendance.

The church bell was rung for the first time in 1887, the first wedding was held in 1891, and the first full-time minister was hired in 1915. Sunset Congregational Church joined the United Church of Christ in 1957.

HISTORY

In addition to the Martha Washington Benevolent Society, other women's groups were formed in the Sunset Church. In 1908, the Sunset Sewing Circle was formed, and in 1915, it dissolved. In 1915, the Church Aid Society was formed. Its purpose was to help the church socially and financially. Members in it were active, and membership in it was honorary. This group plays a vital role today in the church.

The Choir and the Organist of the Sunset Congregational Church also play an important role. In 1984, there were four members in the choir, and they would meet with the organist forty-five minutes before each service to decide on the music that would be used. Today there are approximately fifteen members in the choir, which grows during the summer months when the summer residents are present. The music of the choir lifts the spirits and forms a bond among the church members. The choir and organist set the tone for the congregation and demonstrate commitment, love, and joy. They communicate to all who are present that they are sitting in a very special place.

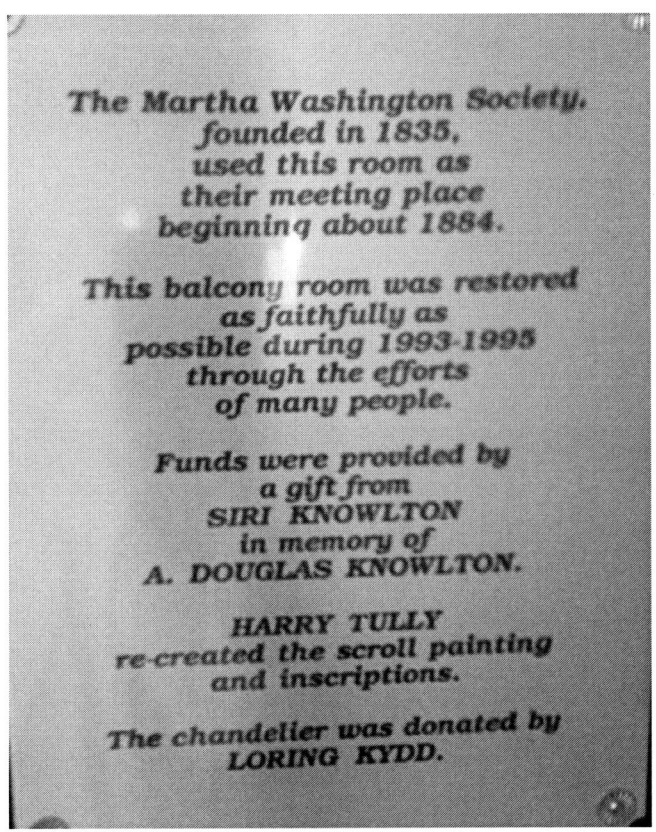

The children of the church always have been a focal point of Sunset Congregational Church. Each May, the children give a performance during the church service as their end of year event. During the summer months, they meet in the Parish House for special activities during the church service. They are excused to go to the Parish House after Time With Children during the regular service. Occasionally, they have been asked to come to the altar during the regular church service to participate in christenings.

The Sunday School has met in three places throughout the history of the church. It has met in the Balcony. It has met in the Vestry, which was bought in 1915 and sold in 1943, and it has met in the Parish House.

The first full time minister was hired in 1915. He served both the Deer Isle and the Sunset Parishes. He traveled between them with horse and carriage or sleigh when it was needed. Church records show the following Roster of Pastors for the Sunset Congregational Church:

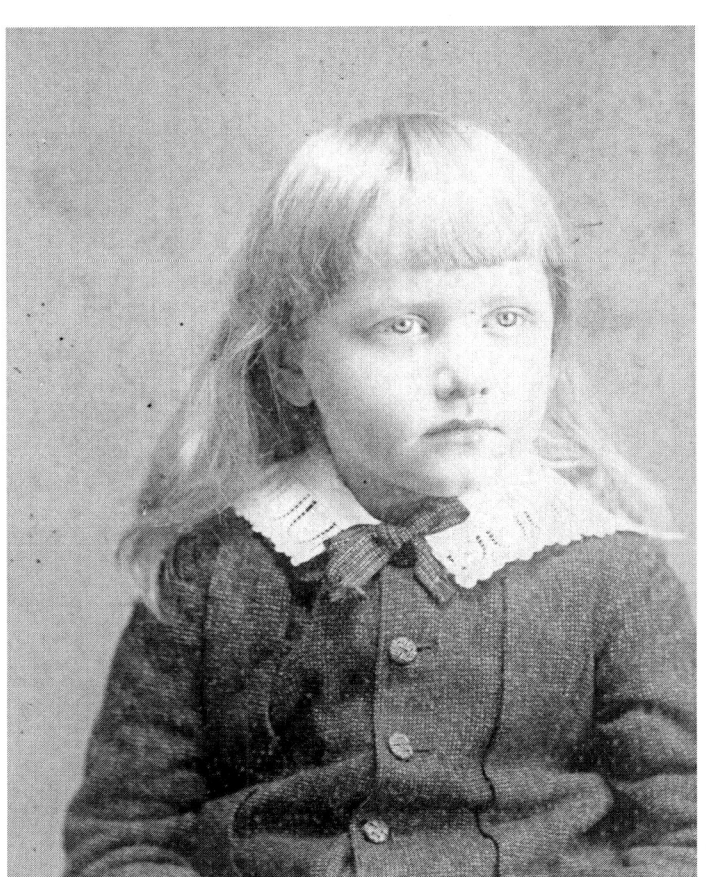

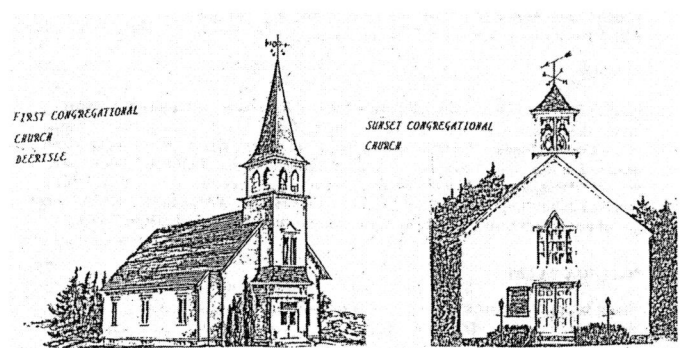

Part-time Ministers
Howard W. Collins	1912
John W. Threlfall	1912
Harry Barrass	1913 - 1914
S. Gordon Tucker	1914

Full-time Ministers
Orville J. Guptill	1915 - 1919
William L. Jennings	1919 - 1921
William N. Bessey	1922 - 1923
Walworth Tyng	1923
John F. Snyder	1924
Inor Partington	1925
Frank A. Judkins	1926 - 1935
Ralph H. White	1935 - 1938
Frank E. Ratzell	1938 - 1942
Edward L. Manning	1942 - 1947
Robert A. Snelling	1947 - 1950
Herbert Brewster	1951 - 1954
Glen E. Rodgers	1954 - 1958
Paul K. Whiting	1958 - 1959
Donald L. Elliott	1959 - 1963
Charles A. Separk	1964 - 1966
J. Owen Speaker	1967 - 1988
Howard Haskell Tobak	1988 - 1989
Peter Baldwin Panagore	1989 - 1993
Suzanne M. Zacher	1993 - 1995
Roger Samuel Burkhart	1995 - 2003
Alice A. Hildebrand	2004 - 2011
Dana Douglass	2011 - Present

The Pastors have shepherded and led the congregation for 100 years. They have helped it form a new relationship with the First Congregational Church of Deer Isle as the two churches merged in 2010. Today the church is known as the Deer Isle-Sunset Church, UCC (United Church of Christ). During the winter months of October through May, the congregation meets at the Deer Isle Church, and during the summer months of June through September, the congregation meets at the Sunset Church. The Sunset Church enjoys a boost in its attendance from the summer residents who help to support the combined congregation financially, emotionally, and socially. The first two centuries of the First Congregational Church of Deer Isle were chronicled in the 1973 edition of Hugh B. Frey's *Two Centuries*, the History of the first Congregational Church of Deer Isle, Maine. The first century of the Sunset Congregational Church has been summarized in this edition. The uniting of the two churches will be told in the story of the next 100 years.

"And now old Comrades of the Martha Washington Temperance and Benevolent Society who have rounded the century mark with thinning ranks but with redoubled courage, to you belongs not only its past but its future. That past has built itself into memory around us. It has left a memorial that shall never perish while this green earth shall roll. You may fold the busy hands and close the book, but its record can never be forgotten. As long as Death can enter into a household in this community, the memory of what this Society has done for it must go with it."

Miss Frances L. Hosmer
"Early History of The Martha Washington Benevolent Society," written at the age of 92 years old for their Centennial, 1935.

Church Aid Society making balsam fir pillows

" Cooking is like love; it should be entered into with abandon or not at all."

Harriet van Home

Chapter 1

SALADS

Psalm 145:15
The eyes of all look to you, and you give them their food in due season.

Periwinkle Orange-Pineapple Salad

1 pkg orange gelatin
20 oz can crushed pineapple
8 oz cottage cheese
12 oz whipped topping (i.e. Cool Whip)

Combine the gelatin, crushed pineapple (drained) and cottage cheese and stir well. Fold in Cool Whip. Chill and serve

Serves 6 - 8.

Neva Beck

This easy recipe can be served as either a salad or a dessert. I've often served it at family dinners as well as Ladies Aid Luncheons. Mrs. Beck has been the proprietor of The Periwinkle in downtown Deer Isle for 45 years. In addition to autographed books by local authors, children love her penny candy, and adults admire the hand-woven wool rugs she makes over the winter.

"Why go West when Maine has everything?"

Henry David Thoreau

Cabbage Crunch Salad

1/2 medium head of cabbage, shredded
4 green onions, chopped
2 T sunflower seeds
1/2 cup slivered almonds
1 pkg chicken flavored ramen noodles

Dressing:
2 T sugar
1/2 cup oil (recommend safflower)
3 T red wine vinegar
1/2 tsp pepper
1 pkg chicken flavoring from ramen noodles
1 tsp salt

Dry roast sunflower seeds and almonds at 350º for 8 minutes.

Add sunflower seeds and almonds, 1 pkg chicken flavored ramen noodles (uncooked) and broken to make crunch. Mix with dressing, cabbage and onions 1/2 hour before serving.

Serves 4

Nell Holder

Sunset Chicken Summer Salad

2 chicken breasts
1/2 cup mayonnaise
1/4 cup sweetened dried cranberries
1/4 cup chopped celery
1/4 cup sunflower seeds
2 T chopped onion
2 T shredded carrot

Cook chicken breasts with seasoning of your choice. Cool and cut into bite size pieces. Add dried cranberries, celery, onion, carrots and sunflower seeds. Blend in mayonnaise which allows the flavor of the ingredients to remain prominent.

Simple, easy and yummy.

Serves 4

Pat Wiegand

"Every day we decide who we will be by the actions we take."

Jazzy Black Bean Salad

15 oz can black beans
1 1/2 cups frozen corn
1/2 cup green onions or shallots, chopped
1 whole pickled jalapeno pepper, minced (not seeded)
3 fresh plum tomatoes
1 avocado
1/2 cup fresh chopped cilantro
1/4 cup chopped basil
1 T lime juice
1 T olive oil
1/2 tsp sugar, to taste
Salt and pepper, to taste

Rinse and drain black beans. In a large bowl, combine beans, corn, onions, jalapeno peppers, tomatoes (seeded and chopped), avocado (cut into chunks), cilantro, basil, lime juice and olive oil. Add sugar, salt and pepper to taste (the sugar helps balance the acidity from the tomatoes and lime juice).

Chill before serving.

Serves 6 - 8

Del Rosenfield

Orange-Pineapple Salad

6 oz pkg orange gelatin
15 oz can crushed pineapple
6 oz pkgs cream cheese
3 large carrots, cut in chunks

Put gelatin and cup of hot water in blender and pulse. Add to reserved juice enough water to make 3/4 cup of liquid; add and pulse. With blender on low, add cream cheese, pineapple drained (save the juice) and carrots.

Pour into 2 quart mold. Chill until firm.

Serves 4 - 6

Norma V. Sheard

"Enjoy the little things in life, for one day you may look back and realize they were the big things."

Island Chicken Salad

2 cup diced cooked chicken
1 can hearts of palm
1/3 cup chopped onion
1/3 cup chopped celery
1 cup red seedless grapes, halved
1/2 T curry powder
1/2 cup mayonnaise
1/2 cup sour cream
1/2 cup mango chutney

Mix together curry powder, mayonnaise, sour cream and mango chutney.

In separate bowl mix chicken, hearts of palm (drained and chopped), chopped onion, chopped celery and red seedless grapes in a large bowl.

Add sauce mixture, cover and refrigerate to blend flavors before serving.

Serve on a bed of lettuce with tomato and avocado slices.

Serves 4 - 6

Bill & Marsha Johns

Karen's Broccoli Salad

2 cups broccoli florets
1 1/2 cups shredded extra sharp cheddar cheese
1/2 cup bacon
1 red onion (small)
1/3 cup raisins

Dressing:
3/4 cup mayonnaise
1/3 cup sugar
2 T cider vinegar

Cook bacon and crumble into small bits. Dice onion. Combine bacon and onion with dressing and toss with broccoli, cheese and raisins.

Easy, colorful, and delicious.

Serves 4 - 6

Carol Bischoff

I got the recipe from our daughter-in-law, Karen Davis, who often takes this to the teacher luncheons in Manchester, NH.

Autumn Island Salad

1 1/2 lbs fresh green beans
1 cup toasted walnuts
1 cup red or Vidalia onions
1 cup feta cheese
Mint leaves to garnish

Mint Dressing:
3/4 cup olive oil
1/2 cup chopped mint leaves
1/4 cup white wine vinegar
3/4 tsp salt
2 garlic cloves, minced
1/4 tsp white or black pepper

Parboil fresh beans (halved) for 3 - 5 minutes. Chill to stop cooking and drain on towel.

Arrange beans on salad plate and sprinkle with walnuts (chopped), onions (diced) and crumbled cheese. Garnish with mint leaves.

Whisk or blend all dressing ingredients together.

Drizzle dressing over salad and pass the rest.

Serves 6

Shirley Banner

I like this in the spring with sugar snap peas also.

Brook Cove Bean Salad

1 can (16 oz) kidney beans
1 can (15 oz) black beans
1 can (15 oz) garbanzo beans
2 celery ribs
1 red onion (medium)
1 tomato (medium)
1 cup frozen corn, thawed and drained on towel

Dressing:
3/4 cup thick and chunky salsa
1/4 cup vegetable oil
1/4 cup lime juice
1 1/2 tsp chili powder
1 tsp salt, optional
1/2 tsp ground cumin

In a bowl, combine beans (rinsed and drained), sliced celery, diced onion, diced tomato and corn.

Dressing: In a small bowl, combine salsa, oil, lime juice, chili powder, salt and cumin. Mix well. Pour over the bean mixture and toss to coat.

Cover and chill for at least 2 hours.

Serves 10

Patty Gillett Elliott

This is a zippy, colorful salad, and an alternative to 3-bean salad.

Curried Brown Rice Salad

4 cups cooked brown rice
1 cup chopped unpeeled tart apple
1/2 cup raisins
1 dash onion powder
1/2 cup slivered almonds
1/2 cup reduced-fat mayonnaise
1/3 cup fat-free plain yogurt
3 tsp curry powder
1/2 tsp salt
Peas, frozen or fresh (optional)

In a large bowl, combine the rice (cooled), apple, raisins, onion powder and almonds.

Dressing: In another bowl combine mayonnaise, yogurt, curry powder, salt and peas. Pour over rice mixture and stir to combine.

Refrigerate for at least 1 hour before serving.

Makes 6 cups

Carlee Min Davis

I adapted this recipe by usage. I always add frozen peas to add color, flavor, and texture. I sometimes add more apple and raisins. I also use vanilla yogurt since I don't often have the plain on hand, so it makes it a bit sweeter, but with only 1/3 cup it's not a big impact.

Eggemoggin Salad

1 lb extra firm tofu
1 grated carrot
1/2 cup celery
1/4 cup onion, chives, or green onions
2 tsp Dijon mustard
2 tsp turmeric
1 tsp cumin
2 T fresh parsley
Salt and pepper
1/2 cup light mayonnaise
Lettuce

Place tofu in boiling water to cover. Boil 10 minutes. Cool. Mash tofu with fork. Add grated carrot, finely chopped celery, finely chopped onion (or chives or green onions) into tofu. Stir well. Add Dijon mustard, turmeric, cumin, chopped parsley, salt and pepper to taste to tofu mix. Add enough mayonnaise to hold mixture together.

Chill for 1 hour. Serve on lettuce or as sandwich filling.

Serves 4

Ann Hooke

"It's never too late to become who you always wanted to be."

George Elliot

Green Dream Salad

1 pkg lime gelatin
1 cup low fat cottage cheese
1 cup crushed pineapple, drained

Make the gelatin according to the package directions using the drained pineapple juice as part of the cold water. Chill just until thick. Add cottage cheese and pineapple and stir well. Pour into a clear mold so you can appreciate the "green."

Refrigerate until set. Serve on lettuce.

Serves 4

Diana Davis

The amounts of cottage cheese and crushed pineapple can be varied according to taste or what you have on hand.

This is a recipe my Grandma Bischoff in Nebraska always made when we went to see her. It was a standard at their church dinners, especially in the 1970's. She called it Lime Jello Salad, but I renamed it and this seems much more appealing. My mom always makes sure we have it at least once when I am home, and now the grandchildren also love it.

Broccoli Slaw

12 oz. cello pkg broccoli slaw or slivered broccoli
1 Granny Smith apple
1 cup red seedless grapes
2 cups mandarin oranges

Sweet onion dressing:
1 1/2 cups canola oil
2/3 cup apple cider
1 large sweet onion
1 clove garlic
1/2 cup granulated white sugar
1/2 tsp ground mustard
1 tsp salt

Stir together broccoli slaw or slivered broccoli, apple cut into small wedges, halved grapes, and drained oranges. Chill before serving.

Dressing: Place canola oil, apple cider, crushed garlic, peeled and chunked onion, sugar, mustard and salt into blender and blend until smooth.

Makes about 3 cups. That's enough to have some dressing left over for other salads.

Sally T. Gillett

It was cool and refreshing when served by southern friends, in the winter in Florida.

Cranberry Spinach Feta Salad

8 oz fresh spinach or baby spinach
1/2 cup feta cheese
1/4 small red onion
1/2 cup dried sweetened cranberries
2 T toasted sliced almonds (optional)

Dressing:
1/2 cup balsamic vinaigrette
2 T orange juice
1 tsp orange zest, optional

Add half of crumbled feta cheese and all of the thinly sliced red onion to spinach and toss to combine.

Dressing: Combine balsamic vinaigrette, orange juice and orange zest. Pour over salad and toss to coat.

Sprinkle with remaining cheese and top with cranberries and almonds.

Serve immediately.

Serves 4

Judy Rittmeyer

Easy Corn Pea Salad

1 can French style green beans
1 can small peas
1 can shoe peg corn
1 small can pimentos
1 onion
2 stalks celery
1/2 cup vinegar
1/2 cup sugar
1/2 cup vegetable oil

Drain cans of vegetables, add pimentos, sliced onion, and chopped celery. Add salt and pepper to taste.

Dressing: In sauce pan, bring to a boil the vinegar, sugar, and oil. Cool. Pour over mixed vegetables.

Serves 4 - 6

Dottie Bonnet

Fresh vegetables, cooked minimally, would also be good in this.

"Explore, Dream, Discover!"

Mark Twain

Northeast Cabbage Salad

1 head of Napa or Chinese cabbage, chopped
1 head of chopped broccoli florets
2 - 3 chopped scallions
6 T margarine
2 pkgs ramen noodles
1/2 small jar sesame seeds
1 small bag slivered almonds

Mix well in shaker:
1/4 cup olive oil
1/4 cup sugar
Soy sauce, to taste (use 2 - 3 tablespoons)

Mix together cabbage, chopped broccoli florets and scallions. Toss and chill.

Sauté with margarine, ramen noodles (broken into small pieces), sesame seeds, and slivered almonds until golden. Let cool.

Dressing: Mix olive oil, sugar and soy sauce.

Add cooled mixture to chilled mixture and toss with dressing.

Toss 1 to 2 hours before serving, toss again before serving.

Serves 6 - 8

Leona Miller

This is a favorite. Napa cabbage is often a very large head and I have asked grocery store vegetable department people to cut it in half and wrap it for sale. It sells by the pound and they'll gladly do this so you don't have to eat it for a week, but it's also a great dish to share.

Carottes Aux Chalets Français

1 1/2 cups plain lowfat yogurt, drained to thicken.
1 cup walnut pieces, shells removed
2 lbs carrots, peeled and cut
1/2 cup fresh mint leaves, snipped small
2 T honey
1" ginger root, peeled
1 cup golden raisins

Get food processor out.

The night before or 8 hours before, line a sieve with a paper coffee filter and set over a bowl. Place yogurt in lined sieve, cover and refrigerate for 8 hours. You may need to drain whey (liquid) from bowl occasionally.

Preheat oven to 350°.

Place walnut pieces in a baking pan and toast until golden brown and fragrant, about 7 minutes. Allow to cool slightly. Process toasted nuts in work bowl with metal blade a few pulses until coarsely chopped. Set aside. Insert shredding disc. Place carrots in the large feed tube horizontally and shred. Transfer to a large mixing bowl. Insert metal blade and process ginger root until finely chopped, about 5 to 10 seconds. Scrape bowl. Add thickened yogurt, mint and honey. Process to combine with a few pulses. Scrape the bowl and pulse about 5 seconds more. Add to shredded carrots and combine. Add raisins and gently mix. Serve chilled on a bed of lettuce. Yum!

Serves 4 - 8

Cheryl Davis Norton

I sometimes use almond slivers, dried sweetened cranberries and 8 oz drained crushed pineapple, omitting the ginger, walnuts and raisins. A very different taste.

Lobster & Wild Rice Salad

3 1/2 cups cooked wild rice
2 cups cooked lobster meat in bite-sized chunks
2 medium-sized avocados
1 T lemon juice
1/2 cup coarsely chopped red onion
1 T Dijon mustard
2 1/2 T red wine vinegar
1/2 tsp minced garlic
1/2 cup extra virgin olive oil
Salt and freshly ground black pepper to taste
1/4 cup chopped fresh parsley

Combine cooled rice, lobster and red onion in large bowl. Peel avocados and cut in chunks. Sprinkle with lemon juice to prevent discoloration. Add avocados to bowl.

In a small bowl, whisk together the mustard and vinegar. Gradually whisk in the olive oil. Add garlic, salt, pepper and parsley. Mix well and pour over salad. Toss.

Serve at room temperature on bed of greens.

Basic Wild Rice:
Combine 1 cup wild rice, 1 1/2 tsp salt and 3 cups water in a heavy sauce-pan. Bring to boil. Cover tightly and simmer over low heat for 45 - 60 minutes until rice is puffed. Drain.

Can be made in advance and travels well.

Serves 4

Bob & Kellie Coombs

Downeast Mandarin Orange Salad

3 cups spinach or romaine lettuce
3 cups iceberg lettuce
11 oz. can mandarin oranges, drained
1/2 cup slivered almonds
2 - 3 stalks celery, sliced

Dressing:
1/3 cup cider vinegar
2 T white sugar
1/2 cup olive oil
1/2 cup fresh mint
Dash hot pepper sauce

Make dressing 2 hours before salad and chill. Mix salad ingredients and add dressing just before serving.

Serves 6

Note: The nuts can be dry roasted and tossed with Tamari soy sauce when still warm.

Judy Stevens

Broccoli Peanut Salad

3 broccoli crowns
1 cup raisins
1 cup salted roasted peanuts
1/2 lb bacon
1 cup mayonnaise
2 T white vinegar
2 T sugar

Mix together broccoli crowns cut into small pieces, raisins, roasted peanuts, cooked and crumbled bacon, mayonnaise, vinegar and sugar. Let chill.

Serves 6 - 8

Debbie Gillett Hermansen

"Love doesn't make the world go round; love is what makes the ride worthwhile."

Franklin P. Jones

Early Spring Cheese Salad

4 cups fiddlehead ferns or fresh asparagus
3/4 lb butter head or bibb lettuce
2 small ripe pears
1/2 cup walnuts
1/2 cup feta cheese or blue cheese, crumbled

Shallot dressing:
2 T lemon or lime juice
1/2 cup olive oil
2 tsp sugar
2 - 3 shallots
1/2 tsp salt and 1/2 tsp pepper

Steam slightly the fiddleheads or asparagus cut into 1" pieces. Then chill while prepping lettuce. Tear crisped lettuce in bite size pieces, but save a few nice leaves for the salad bowl. Gently toss torn lettuce, fiddle heads or asparagus, chopped walnuts and cored and thinly sliced pears together.

Dressing: Whisk together lemon or lime juice, olive oil, sugar, minced shallots, salt and pepper.

Add dressing to salad and gently toss to coat. Spoon into salad bowl lime with lettuce leaves.

Sprinkle crumbled cheese and a dash of salt on top.

Serves 6

Shirley Banner

Sometimes I dry roast the nuts, and splash with tamari while still warm.

Family Cabbage Waldorf

3 Red Delicious apples
1/4 cup regular raisins
1/2 cup golden raisins (optional)
3/4 cup walnuts
2 cups celery
2 cups red grapes
1/2 to 1 head green and/or red cabbage,
    thinly shredded or sliced with sharp knife

Dressing:
1 1/2 cup mayonnaise
2 T brown sugar or honey
3 T apple cider vinegar or fresh lemon juice
1 T water

Core and slice apples.

Mix together in 5 quart bowl apples, raisins, coarsely chopped walnuts, chopped celery, seeded and halved grapes.

Dressing: Mix together mayonnaise, sugar or honey, vinegar, and water.

You can serve at room temperature or chilled. Place in pretty serving bowl with large serving spoon for holidays. Pass around or set up on lettuce on small plates.

Serves 6

Charlotte W. Davis

Fixing the salad for Thanksgiving and Christmas with extended family was my job for many years. I loved being with all the women in the busy kitchen. When feeding twelve to twenty Hessers, Snyders and Wakefields we stretched the Waldorf with cabbage to feed them all. Serves many.

German Salad

Salad greens for 4 - 5 servings
1/4 cup sugar
1/4 cup white vinegar
1 egg
4 strips of bacon, cut in small pieces

Wash, spin, crisp and gently tear the greens. Cook bacon pieces until crisp. Drain and set aside; but reserve about 1 T of bacon grease. To the bacon grease, in same pan, add beaten egg, sugar and vinegar mixture, on very, very low heat. Stir until dressing is slightly thickened and lemon color. Cool.

When ready to serve, pour dressing over salad greens, and toss. Crumble bacon bits over top.

Serves 4 - 5

Susan Perez

We double the recipe and have this every Thanksgiving, Christmas and Easter.

"Twenty years from now you will be more disappointed by the things you didn't do than by the ones you did do. So throw off the bowlines! Sail away from the safe harbor. Catch the tradewinds in your sails."

Green Veggie & Fruit Salad

10 oz pkg frozen peas
1 tart green apple
3 green onions
1/3 cup golden raisins
1/2 cup plain yogurt or sour cream
2 tsp horseradish
2 tsp lemon or lime juice
Salt and pepper to taste
4 oz cooked ham
1/4 cup salted cashew pieces

Thaw peas and drain. Chop apples and combine with drained peas, golden raisins and thinly sliced green onions. Set aside in refrigerator.

Whisk yogurt, horseradish, juice, salt and pepper together. Use it to dress the peas, onions, and apples and raisins.

Top with cubed cooked ham and cashew pieces.

Serves 4 - 6

Neva Beck

Harbor Eggplant Salad

1 medium onion
1 1/2 lbs eggplant
2 large garlic cloves
1/4 cup olive oil
3 - 4 tomatoes
15 - 20 Kalamata olives
2/3 cup toasted pine nuts
2 T capers

Wine Vinaigrette:
1/4 cup red or white wine vinegar
1/2 cup olive oil
1/4 tsp paprika
1 tsp freshly ground pepper

Fry chopped onion, eggplant diced in 1/2" pieces, and minced garlic in the olive oil for about 12 minutes. After adding peeled, seeded, and diced tomatoes, cook about 8 minutes more.

Cool somewhat and add seeded and chopped olives, pine nuts and capers.

Dressing: Whisk vinegar, olive oil, paprika and pepper together and toss with vegetables.

Chill salad at least one hour.

Serves 8

Shirley Banner

I like to find interesting bowls for serving. My most dramatic has been in an artichoke.

Heidi's Green Bean Salad

3/4 cup good quality olive oil
1/4 cup sherry vinegar
4 T Dijon mustard
1/4 cup Italian parsley
Salt and pepper, to taste
3 lbs young green beans
1/2 lb Gruyere cheese
1/2 lb mushrooms

Blanch and chill the beans.

Combine olive oil, vinegar, mustard and chopped parsley to make the vinigrette dressing.

Toss beans, vinaigrette, coarsely grated cheese and trimmed and sliced mushrooms together.

Chill and serve.

Serves 16

Eliza Childs

A real crowd pleaser!

Marilyn's Broccoli Salad

2 cups broccoli, raw or blanched, cut up small
1 cup green seedless grapes, cut in half
1 cup red seedless grapes, cut in half
1/2 cup chopped walnuts
1 cup chopped celery
3/4 cup raisins
1 small red onion, chopped finely

Mix chopped broccoli, grapes, chopped walnuts, chopped celery, raisins and finely chopped onion and let set in refrigerator 2 - 3 hours before serving.

Dressing: 1 cup of white salad dressing or mayonnaise, mixed with enough milk so it's like a dressing. salt and pepper to taste

You can "doctor" the dressing up any way you want; I've added garlic before, also fresh dill.

Makes about 6 1/2 cups

Susan Perez

"Don't cry because it's over, smile because it happened."

Dr. Seuss

Musketeers Frozen Slaw

1 head green cabbage, chopped or shredded
1 medium carrot, chopped or shredded
1 medium bell pepper, chopped
1 tsp salt

Dressing:
1 cup vinegar
2 cups sugar
1/4 cup water
1 tsp celery seed
1 tsp mustard seed

Prepare veggies. Mix ingredients together and let stand one hour. Drain off liquid.

On stove top, in sauce pan, bring dressing to boil and boil one minute. Cool and pour over drained veggies and seeds.

Combine, chill, and serve or pack into containers and freeze for fall and winter gatherings.

Serves 8

Marjorie H. Wakefield

This is the ultimate make-ahead winter salad, that I remember from many community and church suppers. Gram Alice, Jo and Aunt Marge were the "three musketeers" of Quiet Valley, and had many adventures, far and wide for scouts, church, and living historical farm. Cabbage is very available in PA and in ME. They would make lots of this salad way ahead and thaw it for large meals.

Sauerkraut Salad

3 cups sauerkraut, drained and rinsed
1 large onion, chopped
2 oz jar pimentos, diced
1 cup chopped celery
1/2 sweet bell pepper, chopped
1/3 cup water
1/4 cup salad oil
1 cup sugar
2/3 cup vinegar

Mix sauerkraut, onion, pimento, celery and pepper in a large bowl. Mix water, oil, sugar and vinegar in a small bowl until the sugar dissolves. Pour over the salad; mix well, cover and refrigerate for 24 hours.

Serves 6 - 8

The stuff that I put on this salad is the same thing I use on mixed cooked beans and other veggies to make three bean-type salads.

A make ahead salad that we often made in the fall.

Charlo Davis

Ship Ahoy Summer Salad

3 heads bibb lettuce
3 sectioned pink grapefruit, reserve 1/4 cup juice
3 cups strawberries

Strawberry vinaigrette:
8 strawberries
1 cup canola oil
1/2 cup apple cider vinegar
1/4 cup reserved grapefruit juice
1/3 cup honey or sugar
1 tsp celery seed
1 tsp paprika

Section the grapefruit, saving some of the juice. Wash and cut strawberries in half. Chill fruit. Wash, spin and crisp the heads of lettuce. When ready to assemble use the outer pretty leaves for lining individual salad plates. Gently tear rest of lettuce and divide pieces between plates, placing it on top of the nice looking lettuce leaves. Top each plate with a portion of the grapefruit sections and halved strawberries, arranged with the strawberries in the center.

Whisk all vinaigrette ingredients together and drizzle some over each salad.

Serves 6 - 8

Shirley Banner

Southeast Hills Cider Salad

1 head romaine or iceberg lettuce
12 plum tomatoes, halved or quartered
1 seedless cucumber, sliced, peeled
2 carrots shredded
1 sweet or red onion, cut in half at the equator
1 cup sweetened dried cranberries
2/3 cup cashews, salted or tamari toasted
1/3 cup bacon bits
2 cup croutons

Apple Cider Dressing:
1/2 cup canola oil
1/3 cup white or brown sugar
1/4 cup apple cider vinegar
1 clove garlic, peeled and minced
1/4 tsp paprika
1/4 tsp salt
1/8 tsp freshly ground pepper

Prepare all ingredients. Think floating on top of the lettuce. Arrange in a large bowl or individual salad bowls in an artistic manner with salad dressing on the side.

Whisk or blend all dressing ingredients together. Serve in pitcher with small ladle or you can toss the salad with the apple cider dressing before serving.

Serves 8 - 10

Any of the salad ingredients, except for the lettuce, are optional. Others by inclination or availability are encouraged. Amounts can always vary. It's that sweet apple cider dressing that I love.

Cheryl Davis Norton

Spaghetti Salad

1 lb thin spaghetti
2 pkg dry Italian dressing mix (.6 oz each)
1 T olive oil
1 bunch broccoli tips
1 lb carrots, sliced (slightly pre-cooked)
2 cucumbers, peeled
1 bunch green onions
2 whole tomatoes
6 oz can black pitted olives, drained (optional)

Dressing:
1 bottle Salad Supreme seasoning
1 T sesame seeds
2 tsp paprika
1 tsp salt
1 tsp poppy seeds
1 tsp celery seeds
1/2 tsp garlic powder
1/4 tsp coarse ground black pepper
1 dash cayenne pepper, to taste
2 T Romano cheese

Break spaghetti in thirds, cook in boiling water and drain. Mix with 1 tsp olive oil. Set aside. Mix the dressing according to directions. Cut vegetables into bite-size pieces.

Mix the Italian dressing, olive oil and bottle of salad seasoning. Combine well. Add to the vegetables and spaghetti; mix all together well. Chill in an airtight container.

Serves 8

Leona Bischoff

Tasty Tabouleh & Parsley Salad

3/4 cup fine bulgur (or toasted cracked wheat)
2 cups cold water
2 1/2 cup chopped parsley
1/2 cup finely chopped green onions
1/4 - 1/2 cup finely chopped mint
1/4 cup olive oil
2 T lemon juice
1 1/2 tsp salt
1/2 tsp freshly ground black pepper
2 firm ripe tomatoes
Crisp lettuce leaves, upon which to serve
4 oz chick peas, drained
1/4 cup lemon juice with 1/2 tsp salt

Place bulgur in a bowl and cover with the cold water. Wash all the parsley well, shaking off the extra water and removing the thicker parts. Chill the parsley before chopping it. Place bulgur in a bowl and add the chopped green onions. Then take your hands and squeeze the bulgur with them so that the grain gets the onion flavor. Chop both parsley and mint and add to bulgur. Whisk the oil, lemon juice, salt and pepper together. Add to the salad and mix well. Peel and seed the tomatoes before chopping, or if not fussy, just dice and add to Tabouleh. Stir in chick peas. Cover and chill before serving, at least one hour. Add lemon juice and salt when serving or pass around in a small pitcher.

Serves 6

Nell Holder

A very traditional Mediterranean type salad.

Chinese Chicken Salad

1 head of cut up iceberg lettuce
2 cups chopped cooked chicken breast
1 bunch chopped parsley
1 bunch green onions
1 cup toasted slivered almonds
1/8 cup toasted sesame seeds
1 can or small bag of fried won ton strips

Dressing:
3 T sugar
2 1/2 tsp. salt
1/2 tsp black pepper
2 T soy sauce
5 T rice vinegar
3 slices of fresh ginger, minced
2 tsp sesame oil
2 tsp hot chili oil
2 T minced scallions
1/2 cup oil

Cut up chicken into small cubes and cook in pan with water until done.

In a salad bowl add the lettuce, chicken, parsley, almonds, sesame seeds and wonton strips. Make dressing by adding first 6 ingredients together and stir over heat until sugar disolves, add last four ingrediences. Shake well and pour over salad and toss.

Serves 6

Anette Jaquette

A great salad for a luncheon with friends.

Eliza, Anna, Maysie Childs, Peter, Sarah, Catherine and Patty Elliott at Salmon Point (1993)

Mayotta and Ed Kendrick

SALADS

Paula McDonald, Mar Chesney, Susan Haris Seater

Anne Douglass and Ken Gillett

Chapter 2

Appetizers

1 Samuel 17:18

Also take these ten cheeses to the commander of their thousand. See if your brothers are well, and bring some token from them.

APPETIZERS

Ode to a Chanterelle Mushroom

Oh, elusive little fungus
Your stealthy habit to hide among us
Your fickle reluctance to show your beauty
For a humble fungus is quite snooty.

We know you reveal your crown so glorious
For which you're gastronomically notorious
During the velvety morning dew
Custom-tailored just for you.

Amidst the rubble of ancient timber
You hide nestled low and limber
Perhaps not mindful of your fate
Delicately sautéed aboard a plate.

'Tis the destiny of your kind
To titillate epicureans sublime
To serve proudly with beef and wine
A noble exit for your brief time.

Tim Vander Mel

Artichoke Dip

4 large whole-wheat pitas
1/2 T butter
1 onion, finely chopped
3 cloves garlic, finely chopped
12 oz jar artichoke hearts in water, drained and chopped
16 oz frozen chopped spinach, thawed
4 oz can roasted green chilies, drained and chopped
2 T olive oil mayonnaise
2 T whipped cream cheese
Juice of 1 lemon
Salt and pepper to taste

Heat oven to 400º

Cut the pitas into 6 to 8 wedges each and separate the layers. Spread on 2 baking sheets and bake at 400º for 5 minutes or until crisp.

Heat the butter in a large skillet over medium heat. Add the onion and garlic and cook for 5 minutes or until softened. Add the artichokes, spinach, chilies, mayonnaise, cream cheese and lemon juice. Cook, stirring often, for 5 minutes or until hot. Season with salt and pepper.

Serve with the pita wedges.

Serves 4

Eliza Spencer

Flank Steak Appetizer

1/2 cup tamari sauce
1/4 cup granulated sugar
2 T sherry or if you wish, a splash more
2 slices of fresh ginger, chopped or about 1 tsp powdered ginger
1 large clove crushed garlic
2 scallions, sliced into discs
1 flank steak (about 1 1/2 lbs)
Horseradish sauce (optional for serving)

Combine all ingredients, except the horseradish and marinate for several hours. You must turn often. Then, barbeque steak about five minutes per side, but do not overcook.

For use as an appetizer, slice the flank steak into thin strips. Roll strips and hold together with toothpicks.

You may serve this with a horseradish sauce.

This recipe serves a few or many, depending on hunger level of your guests.

George and Meredith Palmer

Port Wine Cheese Ball

1 lb cheddar cheese, soft type
1 lb cream cheese
1/4 lb blue cheese
1/4 lb smoked cheese
1 T prepared mustard
1 T onion salt
1/4 tsp garlic salt
Port wine
2 T horseradish sauce
1/2 cup pickled beets finely chopped and drained.
Parsley, chopped (optional)

Mix all the cheese, except 1 cup of cream cheese, with the mustard, onion and garlic salts, and enough Port to soften.

Form into a log or ball and cover with a coating of the 1 cup of cream cheese mixed with the horseradish sauce and chopped beets.

Refrigerate for several hours and dust with finely chopped parsley.

Arrange on a tray with an assortment of crackers, Melba toast, rye or pumpernickel bread.

Serves 16 - 20

Norma V. Sheard

If you think the pinkness of the beets will annoy you, leave them out, or add nuts instead.

Cheese Puff Canapés

3 egg whites
1 1/2 cup shredded Gruyere or Swiss cheese
1 1/2 tsp Worcestershire sauce
1 1/2 T Dijon mustard
3/4 tsp paprika
4 4" squares of bread (crust removed, diagonally quartered)

Preheat broiler.

Beat egg whites until stiff peaks form. Fold in the remaining ingredients except bread.

Toast bread and place quarters of bread on cookie sheet. Spread cheese mixture on bread quarters and place under broiler until cheese is puffed and brown.

Makes 16 pieces

Pat Wiegand

*"One word frees us of all the weight
and pain of life:
That word is love."*

Sophocles

Cheese Spread

8 oz cream cheese
4 oz blue cheese
4 oz spreadable processed cheese
1 T onion flakes, soaked in 1 tablespoon brandy

At least two days before serving, mix all together, but not too well. It should be a bit lumpy. Chill.

Serve with crackers

Makes about 2 cups

Sue Banks

"Do what makes you happy. Be with those who make you smile. Laugh as much as you breathe. Love as long as you live."

Cheesy Chanterelle Mushroom Bake

8 oz pkg cream cheese, softened
1 cup grated Swiss cheese
1/4 cup chopped onion
6 slices of bacon, cooked and crumbled
1/4 cup Chanterelle mushrooms, sliced and sautéed
1/2 cup milk

Blend together all ingredients. Pour into a one-pint baking dish which can be used for serving.

Bake at 400° for 15 minutes.

Serves 8 - 10

Sue Banks

"There is always, always, something to be thankful for."

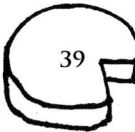

Hot Pizza Dip

8 oz pkg cream cheese, softened
1/2 tsp dried oregano
1/2 tsp dried parsley
1/4 tsp dried basil
1 cup shredded mozzarella, divided
1 cup grated Parmesan, divided
1 cup of pizza sauce
2 T chopped green pepper
2 oz pepperoni, chopped
2 T sliced black olives

In a small bowl, mix together the cream cheese, oregano, parsley, and basil. It helps the flavor to do this a few hours ahead.

Spread the cream cheese mixture in the bottom of a 9" pie plate or a shallow microwave-safe dish or oven safe dish depending on how you decide to cook it.

Sprinkle 1/2 cup of the mozzarella and 1/2 cup of the Parmesan on top of the cream cheese mixture. Spread the pizza sauce over all. Sprinkle with the remaining cheese, then top with the green pepper, pepperoni and olive slices.

Cover and microwave for 5 minutes or bake at 350 degrees for 30 minutes. Serve hot.

Serves 8 - 16

Judy Rittmeyer

I served with bagel chips. It helps to have a knife available for spreading. It is awesome, but with calories!

Chutney Cheese Canapé

8 oz cream cheese, softened
1/4 cup mango chutney
1/4 tsp dry mustard
1 tsp curry powder
Toasted almonds to garnish
Pineapple half (optional)
Crackers

Mix cream cheese, mustard and curry together and then add the chutney. Chop the chutney if some of the pieces are large. Put toasted almonds on top and serve with crackers after chilling.

For a fancy presentation, fill a scooped out pineapple half with the mix and serve with crackers.

Serves 8

Sue Banks

APPETIZERS

Island Crab Dip

1/2 lb prepared crabmeat
2 T lemon juice
2 T horseradish
1 1/2 cups mayonnaise
1/2 cup crumbled blue cheese
Freshly ground black pepper to taste

Fork together and place in bowl. Dip veggies, crackers, chips, or bread.

Serves 8

Charlo Davis

"For a spicy aroma, toss dried orange or lemon rinds into the fireplace."

Curry Paté

6 oz pkgs cream cheese
1 cup grated cheddar cheese
2 T sherry
1/2 tsp salt
1/2 tsp curry powder
1 small jar mango chutney
1/3 cup sliced green onions
Melba rounds

Mix the cream cheese, grated cheddar cheese, sherry, salt and curry powder together with an electric mixer. Form this mixture into a mound on a plate. Pour 1 jar of mango chutney over the mound and sprinkle 1/3 cup sliced green onions over all.

Serve with Melba rounds.

Judy Rittmeyer

"Add raw rice to a salt shaker to keep it flowing."

Deviled & Angel Eggs

Deviled stuffing:
2 tsp onions, grated or finely chopped (optional)
1/3 cup mayonnaise
1 1/2 tsp spicy brown or yellow mustard
1/2 tsp salt
1/8 tsp pepper
1/4 tsp each celery salt & horseradish (optional)
1 tsp worcestershire sauce, or vinegar
1/8 tsp tabasco (optional)
Paprika
Parsley or capers for garnish (optional)

Angel Stuffing:
2 tsps onions, grated or finely chopped (optional)
1/3 cup mayonnaise
1/4 tsp curry powder
1/4 tsp ground cumin
1/2 tsp garlic powder
1 tsp sage
3 tablespoons Parmesan cheese to garnish (optional)
Paprika
Cilantro or parsley for garnish (optional)

For either salad style, place the eggs in a medium to large saucepan and cover with cold water. Bring to a boil over high heat, then lower the heat and simmer for 10 minutes. Remove eggs from pan and rinse with cold water until chilled. Peel eggs and slice lengthwise.

Remove yolks and mash them with a fork. Add desired ingredients and mix thoroughly. Taste and adjust seasonings. Spoon or pipe mixture into egg white halves and garnish with desired garnishes.

Yields 12

Charlo Davis

I like to garnish the deviled eggs with parsley and the angel eggs with cilantro to help differentiate them.

Dijon Mustard Green Onion

1 cup mayonnaise
1/2 cup grated Parmesan
2 T Dijon mustard
Green onion to taste
Olives to taste

Mix together mayonnaise, Parmesan and mustard. Spread 2 tsp of mixture on slices of French bread. Broil until lightly browned. Garnish of green onion can be put on before broiling, and olives afterwards.

Yields 40 appetizers

You can make the mayonnaise, Parmesan and Dijon mixture ahead and keep it covered in the refrigerator for almost a month.

Sue Banks

"Separate stuck-together glasses by filling the inside one with cold water and setting them in hot water."

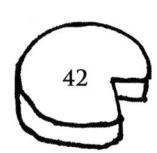

Easy Spinach Dip

10 oz frozen chopped spinach, thawed and well drained
1 1/2 cups sour cream
1 cup mayonnaise
1 pkg dry vegetable soup mix
1 cup water chestnuts, finely cut (8 oz)
2 scallions, finely cut
Loaf round bread

Combine all ingredients except bread and mix until soup mix is well blended.

Let set in refrigerator for 24 hours.

Serve in bread bowl, using inside of bread cut into pieces as "dippers."

Serves 8 - 10

Pat Wiegand

Gorgonzola Walnut Rounds

1 French bread baguette, frozen
1/2 cup olive oil
2 T chopped fresh basil, or 2 tsp dried basil
3 garlic cloves, minced
1/4 lb walnuts
1/3 lb Gorgonzola cheese, crumbled
Fresh basil leaves for garnish

Preheat oven to 300°

Slice the bread in 1/4" slices. Combine the olive oil, basil, and 2 of the garlic cloves. Reserving 1 tablespoon, brush this mixture on one side of each bread round. Bake until golden brown.

Increase oven temperature to 350°.

In a food processor, blend walnuts, 1 garlic clove, and reserved oil until it reaches a paste-like consistency. Spread 2 tsps on the untoasted side of each bread round and top with crumbled cheese. Place in oven and bake until the cheese bubbles. Sprinkle with chopped basil.

Makes 2 - 3 dozen

Sarah Jaquette

Horseradish Dip

8 oz block cream cheese
2 T horseradish
1 T sugar
Mini pretzels

Beat the horseradish, sugar, and cream cheese together until creamy.

Refrigerate overnight.

Serve with mini pretzels.

Makes 1 cup

Jeannette White

"Alone we can do so little; together we can do so much."

Helen Keller

Hot Cheese Cracker

2 cups flour
2 tsp red pepper
2 cups grated cheddar cheese
1 cup melted butter
2 cups crispy rice cereal

Heat oven to 350°.

Combine flour, pepper and grated cheese with melted butter. Add rice cereal. Mix well and form into balls.

On ungreased baking sheet, flatten with fork and bake for 10 minutes at 350° on lower shelf. Turn over and bake an additional 10 minutes.

Serves 8

Pat Wiegand

Mini BLTS

12 cherry tomatoes
3 strips bacon
1 1/2 cups chopped lettuce (red or bibb are best)
1 T mayonnaise

Cook bacon crispy and cut into little pieces.

Slice off bottom third of tomatoes and scoop inside out with a melon baller. Turn tomatoes upside down to drain on paper towel or rack.

Put bacon, lettuce and mayo (just enough to hold it together) in a bowl. Then divide between the tomatoes and stuff it in them. Serve from buffet or pass among guests.

Serves 6

Meghan Wakefield

Pesto Dip

3/4 cup dried parsley
4 tsp dried basil
2 medium garlic cloves, minced
1/2 cup light olive oil
1/2 cup Parmesan cheese

Mix all in blender.

Yummy on crackers or in mushrooms.

Serves 8 - 10

Pat Wiegand

"The fine art of life is to make another soul vibrate with a song of joy."

Edwin Leibfreed

Shore & Hen House Quiche

1 9 inch frozen pastry shell or 24 miniature shells
1/2 lb cooked and peeled Maine shrimp or crabmeat
2 tsp lemon juice
3 large eggs
1 1/2 cups half-and-half or 12 oz evaporated milk
1 T cornstarch
1 tsp salt
1/8 tsp pepper
1/2 tsp dill weed, dried or fresh
8 oz package shredded Swiss cheese
1/2 cup green onions
Paprika
Lemon wedges

Heat oven to 375°.

Thaw pastry shell 20 minutes. Toss shrimp with lemon juice and let stand 5 minutes. In medium bowl, beat eggs and stir in half-and-half, cornstarch, salt and pepper, and dill weed until smooth.

In pastry shells layer in order: half of cheese, half of green onions, all of shrimp (drained), remaining green onions and cheese. Slowly pour egg mixture over cheese. Sprinkle paprika over the top.

Bake 40 - 45 minutes, until outer edge comes out clean, but center is still soft. For full pie, cool 20 minutes before cutting into slim wedges.

Serve warm with lemon wedges or refrigerate and serve cold. You can vary this by omitting the lemon and dill weed, using 1 1/4 cups chopped ham.

Serves 24

Charlo Davis

At Haystack Mountain School of Crafts on Deer Isle, they use this recipe and use 1/2 cup black olives, 2 cups broccoli florets, 1 medium chopped onion, and 2 1/2 cups grated sharp cheddar. Very cheesy and yummy.

Vegetarian, Gluten-Free Yummies

1 cup chick pea flour (available at health-food stores)
Enough water to make cake-like batter
1/2 sweet onion, medium size, chopped
Generous handful of fresh spinach, chopped
Sea salt or kosher salt to taste
Dash of red pepper flakes
Canola oil for frying

Combine and mix all ingredients together except the oil.

Meanwhile, in a large (10" or 12") frying pan, heat canola oil (about 1 1/2" deep) over medium heat, to the point where it is just beginning to bubble. You don't want the oil too hot, or to cook too fast, or these yummy treats will be uncooked in the center.

Now, with your floured fingers, form the dough into bite-sized pieces and plop into pan to cook, turning once, and remove from pan with slotted spatula to a paper towel to drain once they are golden on both sides.

Serve immediately and start frying up the next batch.

By the time the second batch is done, your company will have devoured the first batch!

Makes 16

Azra Shah

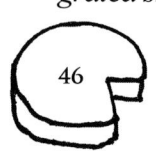

Mom's Crabmeat Dip

1 clove of garlic, cut in half
1/3 cup of cream
8 oz cream cheese
1/2 lb crabmeat
2 tsp lemon juice
1 1/2 tsp Worcestershire sauce
Salt & pepper to taste

Rub bowl with garlic. Add cream cheese and cream, combine. Mix in other ingredients until smooth.

Makes 1 cup

Susan Perez

We always like a little seafood to nibble on when we get together.

Olive and Nut Cheese Ball

8 oz cream cheese, softened
4 oz blue cheese, crumbled
1/2 lb margarine or butter, softened
1/2 cup chopped olives, drained
1/3 cup chopped nuts like pecans or walnuts
Wheat crackers for serving

Mix all ingredients except nuts. Chill and form ball. Roll chilled cheese ball in nuts so it is covered.

Serve with wheat crackers, or rice crackers.

Serves 8

Jeannie Gresham

Shrimp Ball

6 oz can shrimp or two 4 oz cans
1/2 small onion, diced fine
1/4 cup soft butter
1 tsp lemon juice
1/4 cup mayonnaise
1 stalk celery, chopped fine

Mix together all ingredients. Form into ball and chill.

Serve with crackers

Serves 6 - 8

Patty Elliott

"If you're afraid of butter, use cream"

Julia Child

Smoked Salmon Bites

24 oz smoked salmon
Black pepper, grated
Juice of one lemon, squeezed freshly
16 squares of toast or party crackers
3 T Dijon-style mustard
3 hard-boiled egg yolks
2 T mayonnaise
3 tsp fresh dill, snipped
1 medium red onion, diced finely

Diagonally thinly slice salmon, season with pepper and sprinkle with lemon juice. Set aside a moment. Brush toast squares or crackers with mustard and place seasoned salmon on top. Spread smallest swipe of mayonnaise on top of salmon to hold on the garnishes. Extrude egg yolks through mesh of a strainer. Dill and red onion are used to garnish the salmon.

Keep cool until serving, and present on a nice platter.

Makes 16.

Stephen S. Norton

Steve is Charlo's son-in-law, a handy cook and grill master for the Davis-Norton family. These are sometimes served while waiting for the grilled food. Cheryl and Steve had both Nick and Dean baptized at the Sunset Congregational Church.

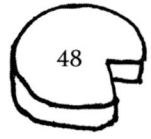

The mission boat "Sunbeam" visits Deer Isle following the Sunbeam Fair. Rev. Haskell receives a donation check from Susie Chesney Wakelin. Also pictured (left-right): Stevie Wakelin, Eric and Timmy Vander Mel, Patty Gillett, David Morrish, Jake Garrels, Jeff Wakelin, Tommy Harrison, Eliza Garrels (1973). The tradition of the Sunbeam Fair originated many years before this photo and continues to this day with the enthusiastic participation of the next generation.

John and Evangeline Bicknell

Bob and Ruth Harris

Tim Van der Mel and Suzanne Decrow

Don Reiman and Brad Pusey

Phil Miller and Jack Scott

CHAPTER 3

SOUPS

Psalm 145:15

The eyes of all look to you, and you give them their food in due season.

Clamdigger Navy Bean Soup

1/2 cup dried navy beans
1 ham bone
1 carrot, diced
1 onion, diced
1 potato, diced
4 cups boiling water
Salt and pepper

Pick over the beans, wash; cover with cold water and soak overnight.

In the morning, add the remaining ingredients and cook slowly until the beans are tender. This will require 2-3 hours.

Remove the ham bone. Press vegetables through a sieve and thin to the desired consistency with hot water if necessary.

Season to taste. Garnish with minced parsley.

Serves 4

Bernard Spofford

This recipe is from the Clamdigger Restaurant on Deer Isle and originated in 1664.

Chilled Cranberry Soup

12 oz big cranberries
3 cups water
1 cup sugar, to taste
2 cinnamon sticks
2 allspice berries
2 whole cloves
4 whole black peppercorns
1 T cornstarch in 2 T cold water
1/2 cup heavy cream
3/4 cup dry red wine
Yogurt (optional)

Pick cranberries over for stems and rinse in cold water. Combine the water, sugar and spices in a large saucepan and bring to a boil. Reduce heat; add cranberries. Gently simmer 15 - 20 minutes until the cranberries are soft and the liquid is well flavored. Mix cornstarch with 2 T cold water to make a paste. Whisk this mixture into the soup and boil for 1 minute. Do not strain. Let soup cool to room temperature, then refrigerate about 4 hours until chilled. Just before serving, stir in cream and wine. Garnish with a dollop of sour cream, plain Greek yogurt or plain yogurt, if desired.

Serves 4 - 6

Notes: Remove cinnamon, allspice and cloves before serving. Can be made up to 48 hours in advance.

Mary Framptom-Price

Black Bean Soup with Garnishes

1 lb dried black beans, rinsed, and soaked for 10 hours or longer in water to cover by at least 4"
6 cups beef broth
28 oz canned tomatoes with their juice, chopped
2 tsp cumin
6 cups water
Freshly ground pepper and salt to taste

Jalapeno Cream:
2/3 cup plain or low-fat yogurt
1 - 2 fresh or pickled jalapenos, seeded and minced
3 T fresh parsley, minced
1 T minced cilantro (optional)

Garnishes:
1/2 cup chopped red onion
1/2 avocado, peeled, seeded and chopped

Drain the beans and put them in a large, heavy pot. Add the broth and water. Bring the beans to a boil, stirring them a few times. Reduce the heat, and simmer the beans uncovered for 1 hour. Stir in the tomatoes with their juice and the cumin, and continue simmering for up to 2 hours or more, or until the beans are soft.

Transfer the mixture to a large bowl and let it cool briefly. Puree the soup in batches in a blender or food processor until it is smooth, returning the puree to a clean pot as you go. Season with salt and pepper. Bring soup to a simmer.

For jalapeno cream, whisk together yogurt, jalapenos, parsley and cilantro (optional). Serve a dollop of jalapeno cream atop each bowl of soup and serve avocado and onion as additional garnishes. Add a salad and bread. The jalapeno cream can be made 1-2 days ahead.

Serves 4

Kenna Haines

Cold Peach Soup in White Wine

2 cups water
5 whole cloves
3/4 cup white sugar
1 cinnamon stick, broken in half
2 tsp cornstarch in 1/4 cup cold water
1 1/2 cups dry white wine
3 lbs ripe peaches or fresh frozen
1 cup heavy cream-optional
1 cup fresh Maine blueberries-optional
Peach slices, blueberries to garnish

Add sugar, cloves and cinnamon to water; bring to a boil; reduce and simmer 10 minutes. Remove from heat and add diluted cornstarch, whipping it into the syrup with wire whisk. Return to heat and bring to a light boil. Remove immediately from heat and stir in wine; refrigerate. Peel peaches and slice. Purée in blender and add to syrup after taking out the cloves and cinnamon. Chill thoroughly. Whisk in cream, if using, and garnish with blueberries, a peach slice and dollop of whipped cream or sour cream (optional).

Serves 2

Margaret Framptom

Celebration Fork & Spoon Soup

5 T butter
3 large onions, thinly sliced
3 quarts broth or water
12 oz elbow macaroni
1 lb 12 oz canned stewed tomatoes with basil
Garlic and marjoram
2 bay leaves, whole
1 tsp thyme, fresh sprigs stripped, when available
15 oz Maine lobster meat or langostinos (small lobster tails) or other solid shellfish
1 lb white Atlantic fresh or frozen fish
1 head escarole, coarsely cut in 1/4 inch slices
1/2 lb sharp cheddar cheese, grated

Saute onion slices in butter in 5-8 quart soup pot until golden. Add broth and heat for 7 minutes. Add pasta and simmer for 15 minutes. Add tomatoes, bay leaves, thyme and seafood. Cook about 8 minutes, covered.

About 10 minutes before serving, remove the bay leaves and add the sliced escarole.

Remove soup from heat, stir in the escarole, taste, and adjust the seasonings.

The cheese goes on top when served and can be added by individuals.

Charlo Davis

The more kinds of seafood used, the more special the result of the blended flavors in the soup, just like the blended voices in the church choir or community chorus.

This is often served for our family's special occasions. It smells heavenly!

Cold Cucumber Soup

3 cucumbers, peeled
8 oz chicken broth
24 oz sour cream
2 tsp white vinegar
2 tsp garlic salt
Chopped chives or parsley, to taste

Purée cucumbers with broth. Remove to a bowl and add the other ingredients. Chill. Serve with chopped chives or parsley.

Serves 6

Sue Banks

This is a very easy, wonderful cold summer soup.

"There are many miracles in the world to be celebrated and, for me, garlic is the most deserving."

Leo Buscaglia

Broccoli, Bean & Cheddar Soup

14 oz can reduced-sodium chicken broth
1 lb broccoli crowns, trimmed and chopped
14 oz can cannellini beans, rinsed
1/4 tsp ground white pepper
1 cup shredded extra-sharp cheddar cheese
1 cup water
Salt to taste

Bring broth and water to a boil in a medium saucepan over high heat. Add broccoli; cover and cook until tender, about 8 minutes. Stir in beans, salt and pepper and cook until the beans are heated through, about one minute.

Transfer half the mixture to a blender with half the cheese and purée. Transfer to a bowl and repeat with the remaining broccoli mixture and cheese.
Serve warm.

Serves 6

Eliza Spencer

Italian Sausage Soup

1 1/2 lbs mild Italian sausage, sliced
2 cloves garlic, chopped
1 large onion, chopped
12 oz can Italian style tomatoes
3 14 oz cans beef broth
1 1/2 cup dry red wine
1/2 tsp crumbled basil leaf
3 T parsley, chopped
1 medium green pepper, chopped
2 medium zucchini, sliced 1/4" thick
3 cups bow tie noodles, uncooked
Grated Parmesan cheese

Sauté sausage, garlic and onions in a large pot until done. Combine all ingredients except the noodles and cheese. Simmer, uncovered, 1 hour. Add water if needed. Add noodles and cook until noodles are tender.

Serve with Parmesan sprinkled on top.

Serves 8

Jerry Schilling

This also makes a wonderful dinner.

Curried Pumpkin Bisque

2 T olive oil
1 cup diced onions
4 minced garlic cloves
1 cup finely sliced celery
1 cup diced carrots
1 can crushed tomatoes (15 oz size)
4 cups vegetable or chicken broth
1 can pumpkin (15 oz size)
1 tsp curry
2 bay leaves
1/2 cup fresh parsley for garnish
1 cup milk – optional

Place olive oil in a heavy soup pot over medium heat. Sauté onions and garlic for 5 minutes. Add celery and carrots to pot. Sauté an additional 5 to 10 minutes. Add tomatoes, vegetable or chicken broth, pumpkin, curry, bay leaves. Bring to boil; then, simmer gently for 15 minutes. Remove bay leaves. You can put soup through blender or use a stir stick to blenderize soup. Stir in milk, if desired.

Garnish with parsley and serve with bread and salad.

Serves 6 - 8

Ann Hooke

Yukon Gold Potato and Leek Soup

2 lb leeks sliced crosswise 1/2" thick (about 3 cups)
3 T butter
1 lb Yukon Gold potatoes, peeled and cut into 1/2"
1/2 tsp celery seed (I always add more as it cooks)
3 cups low-salt chicken broth
Pinch chili powder
1 1/2 cups of milk
1 tsp kosher salt
Pepper to taste

Separate sliced leeks into rings and soak in a big bowl of cool water for a few minutes to let the grit settle to the bottom of the bowl. Scoop them out and drain.

In a soup pot over medium heat, melt the butter. Add the leeks, potatoes, and celery seed and sauté till the vegetables are slightly softened, about 5 min., stirring often to prevent sticking. Add the broth, salt, pepper and chili powder. Bring to a boil over high heat; reduce to a steady simmer over medium low. Cover and cook till the leeks and potatoes are quite soft, about 15 minutes. Stir in the milk; return to a gentle simmer.

Using a potato masher or hand immersion blender, mash/blend until soup is the consistency desired.

Serves 6

Judy Rittmeyer

Birthday celebration at the Spencer Dickinson cottage

Pictured: Dwight Dickinson, Liza Harrison, Sally Thomas, Phelps Brown, Mel and Ned Kendrick, Sammy Thomas, David Harrison, Mayotta Kendrick, Martha Atwood, Helen Atwood, Ginny Atwood, Spencer Dickinson II, Catey Brown, Meredith and Katharine Harrison, Aunt "Tot" Dickinson, Eleanor and Philip Dickinson and Uncle Spencer Dickinson (circa 1948).

Elana Anderson, Scott Miscione, Lucy Vander Mel, Jim Chesney, Claudette Kydd, Jake Garrels, Stephanie Miscione, David Decrow

Dick Bridges and Allen Myers

Chapter 4

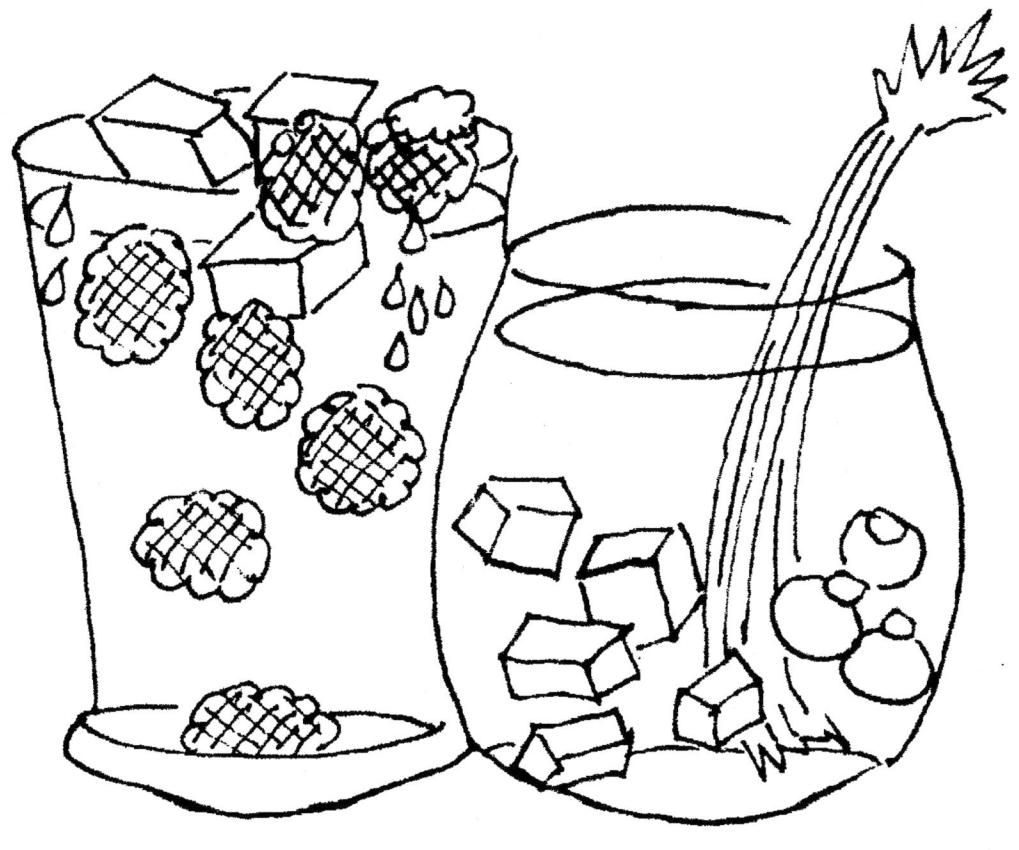

BEVERAGES

Numbers 20:11

And Moses lifted up his hand and struck the rock with his rod twice; and water came forth abundantly, and the congregation drank.

Healthful Green Smoothie

1 banana (the riper the better) cut in chunks
1/2 cantaloupe in chunks
1 1/2 cups unsweetened vanilla almond milk
4 handfuls of fresh spinach
1 cup frozen blueberries
1/2 cup frozen cherries

Put the banana and cantaloupe in a blender. Add the almond milk. Turn on and blend completely. Add spinach. You can start with less but experiment! You will be shocked at how much you can add and it will still be delicious! I probably use about 6 cups of fresh spinach. Blend again until it is completely smooth and you can't see any bits. Add frozen blueberries and frozen cherries. Blend again. To finish, you can sprinkle some chia seeds on top.

Makes 4 cups

Karen Wiens

Dick Davis' daughter, Karen Wiens, is a vegan foodie. Karen's daughter, Stella thought her mom's drink looked interesting, tried it, and loved it. Different and oh-so-healthful!

Hot Orange Tea

4 quarts water
1 tsp whole cloves
1 stick cinnamon
4 family size or 12 individual size tea bags
1 cup sugar
1 cup orange juice, freshly squeezed
3/4 cup lemon juice, freshly squeezed

Put cloves and cinnamon in water and bring to a full boil. Remove cinnamon and cloves with slotted spoon.

Turn heat to low and put the tea bags in the water for 2 minutes (I leave them longer since I like stronger tea flavor). Remove the tea bags and add the sugar, orange juice and lemon juice. Stir until dissolved. Keep hot but do not boil. Serve and enjoy.

Makes 18 cups

You can make half a batch for a great cold weather pick-me-up.

Carol Bischoff

"For tea flavoring, dissolve old lemon drops or hard mint candy in your tea. They melt quickly and keep the tea brisk."

BEVERAGES

Pomegranny

4 oz club soda
2 oz pomegranate juice
1 1/2 oz vodka

Combine and pour over ice cubes. You may adjust amounts to taste.

Makes 1 cup

Lanny Anderson

This recipe was named by Isaac Dworsky.

"Place fresh or dried mint in the bottom of a cup of hot chocolate for a cool and refreshing taste."

Strawberry-Banana Smoothie

10 oz fresh strawberries, stems removed
2 ripe bananas
3 T sugar or honey
3/4 cup milk or yogurt
1 cup ice cubes

Wash strawberries and remove banana peels. In a blender, process all ingredients until smooth.

For a little extra flavor a few drops of vanilla or almond extract may be used. Do not overdo as a few drops go a long way.

Makes 3 cups

Eliza Spencer

"May your love be like good wine and grow stronger as it grows older."

William Graham Harding

Sweet Ginger Tisane

6 cups water
1/4 cup peeled and chopped fresh ginger
1/3 cup fresh lemon juice
1/2 cup firmly packed fresh mint leaves
6 T dark honey
1 lemon, cut into 6 wedges

In a large saucepan over high heat, combine the water, ginger and lemon juice. Bring to a boil; then reduce the heat to low and simmer for 5 minutes. Remove from the heat, add the mint, and let steep for 5 minutes.

Pass the mixture through a fine-mesh sieve, placed over a pitcher, pressing down on the ginger and mint. Discard the mint and ginger.

Stir the honey into the tisane. Serve hot or iced, garnished with a lemon wedge.

Makes 7 cups

Del Rosenfield

This is a delicate, delicious, delightful beverage to serve guests in the afternoon!

Note: Mayo Clinic staff says "a tisane is a soothing drink made by steeping herbs, spices, fruits or flowers in hot water. Here, ginger gives this welcome alternative a pleasant spiciness."

Ash Lane Rhubarb Punch

1 1/2 quarts cubed rhubarb, water to cover
1 1/2 cups sugar or 2 cups local honey to taste
1/2 cup orange juice
2 sticks cinnamon or pieces ginger root
1/8 tsp salt
Water or ginger ale

Cook rhubarb in water to cover, until soft. Strain it through a large fine sieve until you have 5 cups of juice.

Add sugar or honey, cinnamon stick or ginger root pieces and bring to a boil. Take off heat and remove cinnamon sticks or ginger pieces. Stir in orange juice and salt.

Chill or freeze enhanced juice and cover in stainless steel or glass container.

When ready to serve, thaw if needed, then double amount with water or ginger ale. Serve over ice.

Serves 10 cups

Charlo Davis

Blueberry Shrub

1 quart blueberries
1 pint apple or raspberry vinegar
1 pint white sugar, to taste

Freeze 1 cup blueberries or raspberries in ice cubes or place on skewers.

Place the remaining blueberries and vinegar in a 2 quart glass measure. Cover well and chill three days or more. When ready, pour through large fine strainer, press berries to get all their juice.

Pour the strained juice into saucepan. Add the sugar, bring to a boil. Stir occasionally and boil about 3 minutes.

Remove from the heat and cool.

When serving, put 1/4 cup juice into each medium glass filled with ice. Add one cup of cold water. Add berry decorated skewer or straw to stir.

Makes 10

Charlo Davis

Hummm...Red raspberry, white grape and large blueberry for July 4th!

Counterbalance

1 1/2 oz ruby red grapefruit vodka
1 1/2 oz soda water
1/2 lime's freshly squeezed juice
Ice cubes
1 oz Grand Marnier

Pour the first three ingredients into a chilled glass over ice. Then carefully add the Grand Marnier on top.

Makes 1/2 cup

Maysie Childs

This drink puts me and my granny in a very good mood.

"It doesn't matter where you are coming from. All that matters is where you are going."

Brian Tracy

Earl Grey-Type Herbed Ice Tea

1 lime, zested
1/2 cup fresh squeezed lime juice
3/4 cup white sugar
1/2 cup packed fresh tarragon leaves
4 bergamot flavored black tea bags
1/4 cup cold water

Zest just green of the lime with vegetable peeler. Place rind, juice, sugar and 2 quarts water in a pan and bring to a boil while stirring.

Take off stove and let sit for 15-20 minutes. Remove rind. Blend syrup with tarragon in a blender for 30 seconds. Strain through a fine sieve into a tempered glass or container and let chill.

Steep tea bags in boiling water for 6 minutes and then remove. When the tea is cool, stir in the syrup and let chill an hour or more.

Serve over ice. You can freeze a fresh tarragon tip in the ice cubes to garnish.

Makes 8 cups

Charlo Davis

Also good with Duchess Gray and Lady Gray teas. Ever since I worked in the kitchen at Haystack Mountain School of Crafts with Rosemary Forman, I have been inspired to create refreshing summer beverages.

Judge Claybough's Eggnog

10 eggs
3 pints coffee cream
1 pint milk
3/4 cup sugar
1/3 quart (1/3 of a fifth) of brandy
1/3 quart (1/3 of a fifth) of light rum

Beat yolks of eggs until they are light colored. Pour the brandy and rum slowly on the egg yolks, stirring constantly. Then, add the sugar, cream and milk.

In a separate bowl, beat the egg whites until they become very stiff. Lastly, stir in the whites quietly.

The recipe can be weakened with cream.

Makes 5 quarts.

Mel Kendrick

This recipe came to our family in Washington, D.C. in 1921.

Melon Cooler

2 quarts fresh melon
1 T lime juice
1 T granulated white sugar
1 quart club soda or seltzer
2 limes
1/4 tsp salt
2 cups water

Seed and cut melon into 1" cubes. Process melon in food processor or blender with some water, in manageable batches. Drain over a large fine meshed sieve for an hour or so. Press processed melon with a spoon to squeeze more juice from the melon.

Add lime juice, sugar and 1/4 tsp salt and refrigerate until chilled, 1 hour to 5 days.

When ready to serve, place in 10 oz glasses over a couple of ice cubes, add soda and garnish with lime slices.

I make this with cantaloupe, honeydew or watermelon since lime enhances a melon's flavor.

Makes 8 cups

Charlo Davis

I also like to serve and enjoy this as a sauce.

Red Raspberry Limeade

2 cups wild red raspberries
3 1/2 cups water
3/4 cup sugar, to taste
1 cup fresh squeezed lime juice
Mint leaves or sprigs for decoration
2 trays ice cubes made with lime or raspberry juice

Using the food processor or blender process 1 cup of raspberries and 1 cup water together. Use a spoon to push the purée though a fine sieve into a 2-quart glass measuring cup. To this add the rest of the berries and water. Add sugar to taste and the lime juice. Stir it until the sugar grains are dissolved. Place ice cubes into 4 glasses. Add the limeade and garnish the drinks with the mint.

Makes 5 cups

When feeling lazy, and using frozen limeade, I use much less sugar and adjust the water.

Jake Garrels

Our wild red raspberries are so pretty and sweet. They're prized by gulls, bears, squirrels, skunks, deer and us!

Rhubarb Juice

2 quarts rhubarb
2 cups sugar, maple syrup or honey
4 cinnamon sticks or 2 tablespoons
5 cups water
Whole cloves (optional)

Wash and chop rhubarb and place in a seven quart stainless steel pan and add the water. Simmer until rhubarb is soft. Strain the juice, through a large sieve, into a two quart tempered glass measuring cup. Sweeten to taste.

If making spicy, pour the strained juice back into the pot. Place on stove burner. Add cinnamon sticks or whole cloves to the juice and heat to simmer. Without allowing to boil, cook about 5 minutes. Cool and serve.

Makes 2 quarts

Charlo Davis

Rhubarb is a wonderful spring pick-me-up and is easy to grow in the Northeast. Blend with other fruit juices for special treats. An extra benefit is the solid "leftover" rhubarb, which when sweetened, is great as it is.

Adapted from Cheryl Wixson's Ruby Punch.
Used courtesy of Cheryl Wixson, Food Engineer.

Village Green Punch

1 cup sugar syrup
1 cup lemon juice
1 cup lime juice or orange juice
1 quart strong tea
2 quarts white grape juice
1 liter club soda, chilled

Freeze some juice into an ice block. Chill the soda and mix the rest of the ingredients together and refrigerate until ready to set up or put together at last minute by pouring mixture over ice block and adding soda.

Makes 20 cups

Martha Bicknell Goss

"Calorie-free club soda adds sparkle to iced fruit juices, makes them go further and reduces calories per serving."

Outside their meeting hall, now the Sunset Parish House, the "Marthas" are shown demonstrating hand-carding of fleece, spinning on Great Wool Wheels, and winding a ball of yarn from a yarn winder. photograph courtesy Deer Isle-Stonington Historical Society.

BEVERAGES

Lloyd Capen

"How can a nation be called great if its bread tastes like kleenex?"

Julia Child

CHAPTER 5

BREADS

Ezekiel 4:9
And you take wheat and barley and beans and lentils, millet and spelt, and put them into one vessel, and make thee bread of them.

Apricot Bread

1 1/2 cups dried apricots, roughly cut by hand
1/2 tsp baking soda
1 cup sugar
Pinch salt
2 eggs, lightly beaten
2 3/4 cups flour
3 tsp baking powder
1 cup chopped almonds

Heat oven to 350º.

Pour 1 cup boiling water over the apricots and let stand until tender, about 5-10 minutes. Don't oversoak.

Drain and reserve the water. If you don't have 1 cup, add more to it.

Pour reserved water into bowl; add baking soda, sugar, eggs and mix well. Add chopped apricots, flour, powder and nuts; mix again.

Butter and flour two 9"x5"x3" bread pans. Bake in preheated 350º oven for 35 minutes or until risen and browned, or until tooth pick comes out clean. Cool on racks and serve.

Makes 2 loaves

Scarlet Kunst Bennett

All Bran Refrigerator Rolls

1 cup shortening
3/4 cup sugar
1 cup All Bran
2 pkgs yeast
1 cup lukewarm water
1/2 tsp salt
2 eggs, well beaten
6 cups flour (I use half whole wheat flour)
1 cup boiling water

Mix boiling water, sugar, shortening, bran & salt. Stir until shortening is melted. Let stand until lukewarm. Add eggs & yeast softened in lukewarm water. Add flour & beat thoroughly. Cover bowl & place in refrigerator overnight. Make into rolls & let rise until double in bulk.

Bake in a preheated 400º oven for 10 minutes.

Dough keeps well in refrigerator for 5 days.

Anita Melhorn

"To make self-rising flour mix: 4 cups flour, 2 tsp. salt, 2 T baking powder, and store in a tightly covered container"

Beer Batter Bread

3 1/2 cups flour
3 T sugar
2 tsp baking powder
1 tsp baking soda
1/4 tsp salt (optional)
12 oz beer
1 large egg, beaten slightly

Pre-heat oven to 375°.

Mix flour, sugar, baking powder, baking soda and salt in a medium bowl. Add beer and egg and combine well.

Put into well greased 9" x 5" or 4.5" x 8.5" loaf pan.

Bake at 375° for 65 minutes.

Remove from oven and cool on rack.

This is delicious with soup.

Makes 1 loaf

Jackie Dunbar

"When baking in a glass pan, reduce temperature by 25 degrees."

Christmas Bread

2 cups scalded milk
1/2 cup butter
2/3 cup white sugar
2 tsp salt
1/4 tsp freshly ground cardamom seed
1 tsp cinnamon
1/4 cup warm water
2 T yeast (or two pkgs)
2 beaten eggs
8 cups white flour
1 cup golden raisins
1 cup chopped baking cherries
1 cup diced citron

Place scalded milk in a large bowl. Add butter and stir until it melts. Add sugar, salt, cardamom, and cinnamon. Stir well. Allow to cool for 10 minutes. Proof yeast in small separate bowl in the warm water. Add dissolved yeast to large bowl. Stir well. Add beaten eggs to the large bowl. Stir well. Add 4 cups of flour. Stir well and beat until smooth. Add 4 cups flour without stirring. Add raisins, cherries, and citron. Now stir well. Dough will be very stiff. Do not knead. Cover with a dish towel. Let rest in warm place until dough is doubled in bulk (about 2 hours).

Punch down. Turn dough out onto kneading board. Divide dough into 4 equal pieces. Prepare four 4"x 8" bread baking tins by greasing lightly. Knead each dough piece lightly and shape into loaf. Place in tin. Cover with dish towel. Let rise for an hour.

Bake at 350° for 35 to 45 minutes. Watch carefully to prevent burning. Turn out onto rack to cool. Excellent toasted.

Makes 4 loaves

Ann Hooke

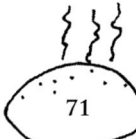

Poppy Seed Bread

1 pkg yellow cake mix
3 3/4 oz French vanilla instant pudding mix
4 eggs
1/2 cup oil
1/2 cup orange juice
2 oz jar poppy seeds
1 cup sour cream or vanilla or lemon yogurt

Heat oven to 350º.

Combine all ingredients and beat with mixer 5 minutes on medium/high. Pour into 2 greased 8 1/2" x 4 1/2" x 2 1/2" loaf pans. Bake at 350º for 40 - 50 minutes or until toothpick comes out clean.

Yields 2 loaves

Lisbeth Nielsen

"When baking bread, a small dish of water in the oven will help the crust from getting too hard or brown."

Norwegian Cracked Wheat Bread

1 T yeast (or one pkg)
2 cups cracked bulgur wheat
2 cups wheat flour
5 cups white flour
1 1/2 T salt
1 cup buttermilk
4 1/2 cups warm water

Place warm water in a large bowl. Add yeast and allow it to dissolve. Stir in the cracked wheat, wheat flour, salt, and buttermilk. Do not knead. Cover bowl with a clean dish towel. Allow to rest for 4 to 8 hours.

Stir in 3 cups flour, one cup at a time until dough has absorbed flour. Gradually add remaining flour until dough is ready to knead. Turn dough onto floured board and knead well for 4 to 5 minutes. Dough will be elastic and smooth. Place dough back in bowl. Cover with dish towel. Let rise for 2 hours.

Turn dough onto kneading board and divide into 4 balls. Prepare 4 bread tins by greasing lightly. Knead each dough ball lightly and shape it to fit into bread tin. Cover and let rise for an additional hour or until doubled.

Bake at 375º for 50 minutes. Cool on rack.

Yields 4 loaves

Ann Hooke

Yorkshire Pudding

6 T drippings from a roast beef
2 eggs
1 cup milk
1 cup sifted flour
1/2 tsp salt

Preheat oven to 450º.

Pour 6 T of beef drippings from the roast into shallow pan (or individual pans) and keep hot.

Beat 2 eggs until light, add 1 cup milk and beat until frothy. Stir in 1 cup of sifted flour and 1/2 tsp salt and beat until smooth. Pour into the very hot drippings and bake in 9" square pan at 450º for 15 minutes. Then reduce heat to 350º for 15 minutes more.

Serve at once with roast beef and gravy.

Serves 8

Note: Ingredients are best if at room temperature.

Norma V. Sheard

This was served in England before the main course. It came from catching the drippings from the roast on the spit. They served it with juice from the meat or gravy.

"When baking bread, you get a finer texture if you use milk. Water makes a coarser bread."

Whole Wheat Quick Bread

2 cups whole wheat flour
1 tsp baking soda
2 tsp baking powder
1 tsp salt

Sift the above into a bowl. Then add:
1/2 cup soy flour
6 T corn oil
1 1/2 cups sour milk
1/2 cup molasses (or honey)
1/4 cup dry milk

Stir well. Spoon into buttered 9" x 5" loaf pan. Let stand 20 minutes.

Heat oven to 350º.

Bake about 60 minutes or until bread is nicely browned and tests done with a toothpick.

Yields 1 loaf

Dick Davis

A lovely bread, especially for breakfast. I made this the first time I visited Carol's house for dinner, a week after we met. She was really impressed that I not only could cook, but that I had made a loaf of bread. I usually add at least 1/2 cup raisins. We've been enjoying it for 27 years!

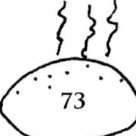

Corn Meal Griddle Cakes

3/4 cup yellow corn meal
2 T shortening
1 cup boiling water
3/4 cup milk
2 eggs, beaten
1 T molasses
1 1/4 cup sifted flour
1 tsp salt
1 T baking powder

Combine corn meal and shortening; add boiling water, cover and let stand 5 minutes. Be sure water is boiling and that all ingredients are well mixed at each stage.

When cool, add milk and eggs. Beat in the molasses and dry ingredients. On a hot, greased griddle, cook large spoonfuls of the batter, turning to brown both sides. These will cook slower and longer than regular pancakes.

Makes 8 griddle cakes.

These are the pancakes that "PopPo" serves to the grandchildren, many of whom have graduated from measuring and mixing to being able to make them for us!

Bob Coombs

"Give us this day our daily bread."

Matthew 6:11

Banana Bread

1/2 cup shortening
1 cup sugar
1/2 cup dark brown sugar
2 eggs
3 very ripe bananas
2 cups all-purpose flour, sifted
1 tsp baking soda, sifted
1 tsp salt, sifted

Preheat oven 350º.

With an electric beater, cream shortening and sugar. Add one egg at a time and beat well. Add mashed bananas. Combine sifted dry ingredients and mix on low until just incorporated. Pour the batter into a buttered and floured bread pan.

Bake 45 - 60 minutes in 350º oven.

Do not remove from oven until toothpick entered in center comes out clean.

Cool 10 minutes. Remove from bread pan to cool on cooling rack, right side up.

Yields 1 loaf

Nancy B Hodermarsky

This recipe comes courtesy of Toshiko Takaezu, a good friend and potter from Cleveland, Ohio and now New Jersey.

Cardamom Raisin Bread

1 quart milk
1 1/2 cups sugar
1 T ground cardamom
1/2 cup butter
2 cakes compressed yeast or two pkg of yeast
1 tsp salt
1 pkg seedless raisins
1 pkg golden or Muscat raisins
2 eggs, beaten
12 cups all-purpose flour

Topping:
1 egg yolk
1 tsp vanilla
1 T sugar

Heat milk and sugar, add butter and cardamom. When butter has melted, cool mixture to lukewarm. Add and dissolve yeast. Add salt, raisins and beaten eggs. Work well together and add enough flour to make a firm but elastic dough. Cover dough and let stand in a warm place until doubled in bulk. Knead well and form into 2 - 4 rounded loaves. Place on greased pie tins or baking sheets and let rise again. Bake at 350° for 1 hour. May need foil cover to protect from burning at end.

Yields 2 - 4 loaves

Katherine Hall Page

This recipe is from my Norwegian grandmother. We've always made it for Christmas. In Norwegian, it's called "JuleKake", meaning Christmas Cake. I now make it all year round.

Cottage Cheese Dill Bread

2 T or 2 pkg dry yeast
1/2 cup lukewarm water
2 tsp honey or sugar
2 cups small curd cottage cheese
2 T minced onion
2 T fresh dill weed, snipped or 1 T dry
2 T granulated sugar
2 tsp salt
1 tsp baking powder
2 eggs
4 1/2 cups unbleached all-purpose flour

In a glass pint container, proof the yeast in the half cup of lukewarm water and sugar until foamy.

In a large bowl, combine and mix well the rest of the ingredients other than flour. Mix well and add sponged yeast. Stir in the flour to make slightly stiff dough. Remove to floured surface and knead about 30 times.

Grease bowl and return dough, covering with moist cloth or plastic. Let rise until doubled. Divide into two medium loaves. Knead again and shape. Allow to rise one last time on baking sheets or in loaf pans.

Bake at 350° for 30 to 45 minutes.

Yields 2 loaves

Meghan Wakefield

A favorite with Marge Wakefield and all her family. A moist bread that is nice with soups or anything.

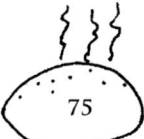

Cuban Bread

1 T salt
1 T sugar
1 pkg yeast
4 - 6 cups flour
2 cups warm water

In a medium size bowl combine the warm water, salt, sugar and the package of yeast; stir in flour. Let rest for 10 minutes. Stir in flour one cup at a time until you have about 6 cups.

The dough will be soft. You don't want it to be very moist or sticky. Cover and let rise in a warm place for approximately 8 hours.

After it has doubled in size, turn dough out onto a floured surface. Divide dough into 2 or 4 pieces, shaping each piece into a loaf shape. Place the loaves onto a baking sheet that is greased and sprinkled with cornmeal. Score each loaf and then brush loaves with water.

Place baking sheet in a cold oven on a shelf above a pan of boiling water. Set oven to 400º and set the timer for 37 minutes. The loaves should be browned somewhat and sound slightly hollow.

Because this bread does not have any fat in it, it does not have a long shelf life. It is best if consumed day one. However, it freezes well so I put the extra loaves in the freezer after they cool. When you need them, thaw and re-crisp the crust in a 300º oven for 10 minutes.

Suzanne Decrow

For the wedding of 50, I made 5 batches, with a basket on each table. See recipes in Celebrations.

Grandmother's Irish Soda Bread

2 cups flour, heaped
1/2 tsp salt
2 tsp baking powder
1/4 tsp baking soda
2 T sugar
1 cup raisins
2 T shortening, melted and cooled
1 cup buttermilk
2 T butter

Heat oven to 350º.

Sift dry ingredients together and add raisins. Mix 2 tablespoons of shortening to a cup of buttermilk. Slowly add this mixture to dry ingredients being careful not to make the dry mixture too soft. Next knead the dough on a floured surface a few times.

Place dough on greased or sprayed cookie sheet. Bake at 350º for 40 minutes, until crust is brown. You can test for doneness with a toothpick. Rub crust with butter immediately as it comes out of the oven. This keeps it soft.

Yields 1 loaf

Judy Stevens

My Grandmother's Irish Soda Bread is a true Irish recipe. My grandmother immigrated from Ireland when she was 18 and my mother made this recipe every Thanksgiving and Christmas and now I do the same. The original recipe is in conversation style with no ingredients separated out, and my mother wrote it as my Grandmother told it to her.

New England Raisin Bread

1 1/2 cups warm milk
1/2 cup sugar
1 yeast cake or 1 T dry yeast
2 tsp salt
4 eggs, slightly beaten
1/2 cup butter melted and cooled, or oil
1 lb box seedless raisins
6 3/4 cups all purpose flour
1 1/2 tsp ground cinnamon (optional)

Mix together milk, sugar and yeast cake. Stir and let sit until yeast foams. Then add salt, eggs and butter. When incorporated, stir in raisins. Mix in flour.

Turn out on to floured board and knead. When earlobe consistency, place in oiled bowls and let rise until about doubled. Divide dough into two loaves. Shape in rounds or rectangles and place on greased baking sheets or in greased loaf pans. Let rise again while oven is preheating to 350°.

When about double, bake for about 45 minutes. Knuckle rap the bottom listening for a hollow sound to know when done. Can brush with egg white before baking, or butter when still warm afterwards.

Yields 2 large loaves

Sandy E. Terrell

I now use the parchment paper or silicone baking mats for no-grease baking sheet preparation. Inspired by Vivian McKenzie of Ware, MA.

Rolled Oats Yeast Bread

1 cup old fashioned rolled oats
1/2 cup molasses
1/2 T salt
1 T shortening or butter
1 yeast cake or pkg
1/2 cup lukewarm water
5 cups flour
2 cups boiling water

Add boiling water to oats and let stand. Add yeast to the 1/2 cup of lukewarm--105° to 115° water. When oats are cooled to lukewarm, add molasses, salt, shortening, dissolved yeast and flour. Combine. Let rise in towel-covered greased bowl for about 3 hours. Knead well, shape into loaves and put into greased bread pans or on parchment covered baking sheets. Put dry towel over and let rise again for about 1 hour. Preheat oven to 375° toward end of hour.

Bake 40 to 60 minutes.

Yields 2 loaves

Marjory Chesney

The vegetable shortening makes a softer textured bread. A favorite of Nancy B. Hodermarsky who contributed Mar's recipe.

Whole Wheat Pizza Dough - Double

2 cup hot water from tap or 105º - 115º
2 pkgs yeast, check expiration date
2 tsp sugar
2 T oil
3 cups whole wheat flour
2 cups white flour
1 tsp salt (optional)
1 cup +/- additional flour to flour rolling surface

Heat oven to 400º.

Mix in bowl 2 cups water, yeast and sugar. Let sit a long time until bubbly.

Mix together with the floor and salt. Knead on floured surface for 15 minutes. Add surface flour, as needed, to keep dough from getting sticky. Then return dough to oiled bowl.

Cover with a cloth and allow to rise to triple in size. Punch out air, cut in 4 pie portions to use then or wrap and freeze.

Roll out a portion of dough to fit circular pizza tray and top creatively with personal choices--see below. Bake in oven for 8 to 20 minutes.

Cut one pie portion into 6 - 8 wedges.

Barbara Alweis

I often had these portions ready to roll out into pizza with my grandchildren who would top them with olive oil and choices of grated or crumbled cheeses, slices of sweet peppers of different colors, zucchini slices, sausage, anchovies, tomato sauce, broccoli florets, sweet onion slices, mushrooms and olives.

Bran Muffins

1/2 cup brown sugar, firmly packed
1/4 cup melted butter
1/4 cup molasses
2 large eggs beaten well
1 cup milk, not skim
1 1/2 cups bran, such as All Bran
1 cup unbleached flour
1 1/2 tsp baking soda
3/4 tsp salt
1/4 cup or more raisins, softened or "plumped" in warm water for a few minutes, then drained.

Preheat oven to 400º.

Mix all together the sugar, melted butter and the molasses. Then add the beaten eggs. Combine the dry ingredients, and add, alternating with the milk to the above mixture. Add the raisins.

Baked in lined medium sized muffin cups for 15 minutes.

Yields approximately 18

Joan Schaum Kendrick

**Betty Brown, Thurston and Woodbury Harrison
Look at those Sylvester Cove flounders!
(approx. 1920)**

Floats from the Deer Isle village annual Fourth of July Parade

After the Fourth of July parade, lunch is served at the OASIS Cafe
in the Deer Isle Sunset Church

CHAPTER 6

COOKIES and BARS

I Samuel 30:12
And they gave him a piece of cake of figs and two clusters of raisins. And when he had eaten, his spirit revived...

COOKIES & BARS

Almond Cookies

2 cups almonds, ground
2 cups raw oats, ground
2 cups whole wheat flour
1 cup canola oil
1/2 tsp cinnamon
1/8 tsp salt
1 cup maple syrup
2 T vanilla
1 tsp almond extract

Heat oven to 350º.

Mix dry ingredients together. Blend wet ingredients. Mix all together. Drop by tablespoon on greased sheet. Flatten with oiled fingers.

Bake at 350º for 20 - 22 minutes.

Yields 2 dozen large cookies

Dan Hadley

Best cookies you ever tasted. I have this easy recipe memorized.

"Tin coffee cans make excellent freezer containers for cookies."

Chewy Maple Cookies

1 cup butter
2 cups brown sugar
2 eggs
1 cup pure maple syrup
1 tsp vanilla extract, or maple extract
1 tsp salt
3 cups flour
4 tsp baking powder
2 cups shredded or flaked sweetened coconut

Heat oven to 350º.

Cream butter, brown sugar and eggs. Beat well. Add syrup and extract and beat well. Add flour, salt and baking powder to moist mixture and mix until blended. Stir in the coconut flakes until just blended.

If using portion scoops use a # 20 (3 1/2 T) for large flat cookies and a # 40 (1 2/3 T) or # 50 (3 3/4 tsp) for medium cookies. They spread well when baking. Dough can be scooped or spooned onto greased baking pans.

Even better, for these very thick taffy-like cookies, is lining the pans with parchment paper or silicone baking sheets to help with easier removal.

Bake about 12-17 minutes until well spread and just done. Place pan on cooling rack and remove cookies with spatula.

Yields 18 large cookies

Joleen Dodge

I sold these at the Four Seasons Stonington bakery and restaurant in Stonington, ME.

Butterscotch Bars

1 cup margarine
1 1/2 cups brown sugar
1 egg
1 tsp vanilla
3/4 tsp salt
1 tsp baking soda
2 1/2 cups quick cooking oatmeal
2 cups flour

Filling:
12 oz butterscotch chips
1/2 tsp butterscotch extract (optional)
12 oz can sweetened condensed milk
1/2 tsp salt
1 tsp vanilla extract
1 cup chopped nuts

Heat oven to 350º.

Melt the margarine; add brown sugar and mix well. Add beaten egg, vanilla and dry ingredients. Mix with a fork; pat half of the crumb mixture into a greased 9" x 13" pan.

Filling: Melt chips, condensed milk, salt and vanilla over low heat, and add the nuts. Pour butterscotch mixture over crumbs; top with remaining crumb mixture.

Bake at 350º for 30 - 35 minutes, until bubbly on the edges and golden brown. Cool and cut into squares.

Yields 40 bars

Carol Bischoff

The recipe was selected for publication by Cooking Light magazine for its Lighten Up makeover in 2009 and they decreased the fat and calories with the result being a more crunchy texture. Our family still gives rave reviews for this "full fat" recipe that came from my mother. The original recipe was for Fudge Filled Cookie Bars and you can substitute chocolate chips for the butterscotch chips and it is also very good.

Bessie Gray's Shed Sugar Cookies

2 eggs
1 cup sugar
1 cup shortening (or 1/2 cup butter, 1/2 cup shortening)
1 T vanilla
Pinch of salt
2 cups flour
2 tsp baking powder

Combine eggs, sugar, shortening, vanilla and beat vigorously. Add dry ingredients and mix together.

Make dough into balls. Flatten, on greased baking sheet, with fork dipped in milk. Sprinkle sugar on top.

Bake 10 minutes at 400º.

Yields 2 1/2 to 3 dozen

Susan Perez

The kids always called these "shed cookies" because Gram always stored her cookies out in the shed!

"A gadget that works well for decorating sugar cookies is an empty plastic thread spool. Simply press the spool in the dough imprinting a pretty flower design."

Diana's Spice Runner Cookies

1 cup unsweetened applesauce
1 1/4 cups packed brown sugar
2 egg whites
1 tsp vanilla
1 1/4 cups whole wheat flour
1/8 cup ground flax seed
1/8 cup wheat germ
1 tsp baking soda
1 tsp cinnamon
1/4 tsp nutmeg
3 cups old-fashioned oatmeal
1 cup raisins
1 cup chocolate chips

Heat oven to 375°.

Blend the applesauce, brown sugar, egg whites and vanilla in mixer. Combine the dry ingredients in separate bowl and then add to mixer. Stir in by hand the raisins and chips.

Shape dough into cookies; we use an ice cream scoop for large cookies. Flatten them since they don't spread during baking. Bake 12-15 minutes, depending on size.

Yields 2 dozen large cookies

Diana Davis

These cookies have NO FAT except for the chocolate chips. They are quite healthful and we often made them for the cross-country running team at Phillips Exeter Academy in NH. We usually double the batch, and to keep it simple, we pour the flax seed and wheat germ in the same measuring cup since the amounts can be varied a bit. Since we like the spices, we often add more cinnamon and nutmeg as well.

Parisian Sweets

1 lb figs
1 lb pitted dates
1 lb raisins
1 lb walnut meats
1/4 cup orange juice
2 tsp salt
Granulated sugar for dipping

Put all fruit and nutmeats through food chopper twice. Add orange juice and salt and mix well.

Roll or pat to 1/4" thickness. Cut in circles with cookie cutter. Roll into balls. Dip in granulated sugar. Shake off excess. Store in cool dry place in a tin.

Ernest Hildebrand

"Cut up dried fruit sometimes sticks to the blade of your knife or food chopper. To prevent this, coat the blade with a thin film of vegetable spray before cutting."

Comfort Cookies

2 sticks unsalted butter at room temperature
1 cup brown sugar
3/4 cup white sugar
2 large eggs, slightly beaten
1/2 tsp vanilla
2 1/4 cups flour
1 tsp baking soda
1 tsp salt
1 1/2 cups semi-sweet chocolate chips
1 1/2 cups butterscotch chips
1 cup coarsely chopped walnuts

Heat oven to 325°.

Cream the butter and sugars together by hand or with an electric mixer. Add the eggs and vanilla. Beat until fluffy.

In a separate bowl, combine the flour, baking soda, and salt. Add to butter mixture and stir or mix well. Stir in the chips and walnuts.

Drop golf ball sized portions onto a non-greased cookie sheet. Bake in a preheated 325° oven for 15 - 20 minutes. Cool on brown paper or racks.

Yields 2 dozen cookies

Katherine Hall Page

I created this recipe just after 9/11. I was having trouble returning to my writing and found that I was doing a great deal of cooking, especially baking, instead. This recipe became a family favorite and one I bring to friends in time of both sorrow and joy now.

Many of us have long enjoyed Katherine's Faith Fairchild Mysteries, some of which take place on a Maine island just like Deer Isle. We have always enjoyed the excellent recipes in her books. She gave us permission to use this one, from her first cookbook, Have Faith in Your Kitchen, published 2010.

Kyra's Lemon Squares

Crust:
2 cups unbleached, all-purpose flour
1/2 cup sugar
1 cup unsalted butter, at room temperature

Filling:
5 extra large eggs
2 cups sugar
5 T unbleached, all-purpose flour
3/4 cup lemon juice
3 lemons grated yellow rind
Confectioners sugar to dust when serving

Preheat oven to 350°.

Place all ingredients in bowl of food processor and process until dough begins to hold together. Transfer to greased 9" x 13" baking pan. Press dough slightly up sides and evenly over bottom of pan. Bake until set and just starting to brown, about 12 - 15 minutes. Remove from oven and cool.

Place eggs and sugar in large mixing bowl. Stir. Add flour 1 T at a time, stirring each addition until well blended. Stir in lemon juice and rind.

When crust is cool pour filling in and bake until just set, about 25 minutes. Don't over bake. Remove from oven and let cool. Dust well with confectioners sugar before cutting.

Kyra Alex

This recipe is a long-time restaurant staple of mine. Is also in my cookbook, Lily's Café Cookbook, Revised Edition by Kyra Alex, 2010. I have given my permission for it to be used here. The squares are often for sale in my Stonington, ME, Lily's Café as well.

Cookie Dough Brownies

Brownie:
2 cups sugar
1 1/2 cups flour
1/2 cup baking cocoa
1/2 tsp salt
1 cup vegetable oil
4 eggs
2 tsp vanilla
1/2 cup chopped walnuts (optional)

Filling:
1/2 cup butter, softened
1/2 cup packed brown sugar
1/4 cup sugar
2 T milk
1 tsp vanilla
1 cup flour

Glaze:
1 cup (6 oz) semi sweet chocolate chips
1 tsp shortening (I sometimes add more if too stiff)
3/4 cup chopped walnuts (optional)

Heat oven to 350°.
In mixing bowl, combine sugar, flour, cocoa and salt. Add oil, eggs and vanilla; beat at medium speed for 3 minutes. Stir in walnuts if desired. Pour into greased 9 x 13 pan. Bake at 350° for 30 minutes or until a toothpick inserted near the center comes out clean. Cool completely.

For the filling: cream butter and sugars in a mixing bowl. Add milk and vanilla; mix well. Beat in flour. Spread over the brownies. Chill until firm.

For glaze, melt chocolate chips and shortening in a saucepan stirring until smooth (I do it carefully in the microwave). Spread over the filling. Immediately sprinkle with nuts if desired, pressing down slightly.

Yields 3 dozen

Carol Bischoff

Gwen's Brambles

1 cup raisins
1 lemon's juice & grated rind
2 saltine squares, rolled to crumbs
1 cup sugar
1 egg
1/4 cup milk
Favorite unbaked pie pastry

Mix together raisins, lemon juice and rind, saltine crumbs, sugar, egg and milk. Place in a bowl and store in refrigerator.

Make your favorite pie crust. You can make it ahead of time. Roll 1/8" thick, cut into 5" rounds and chill until needed, with plastic wrap in between layers.

When ready to assemble and bake, separate rounds, roll pastry on floured surface to 6" diameter. Place 1 tablespoon or more of filling on dough, brush edges with water and fold dough over filling. Press the edges to seal. Form into a slightly crescent shaped turnover.

Place 1 1/2" apart on greased baking sheets. Use a brush to wash with 1 egg yolk, beaten with 2 tablespoons cream.

Bake 20 minutes, or until golden brown at 450°.

Yields 8 - 10

Charlotte W. Davis

Every year Frank's mother made these for a 4th of July treat when the island would, at last, have lemons for sale. Happily, she continued the tradition even when lemons became more plentiful.

Deerfield Sugar and Spice Cookies

3/4 cup shortening
1 cup brown sugar
1 egg
1/4 cup molasses
2 cups flour
2 tsp baking soda
3/4 tsp cloves
3/4 tsp cinnamon
1/4 tsp salt (optional)

Preheat oven to 350º.

Cream together shortening, sugar, egg and molasses.

Sift together flour, soda, salt, cloves and cinnamon.

Mix wet and dry ingredients together and form into walnut-sized balls. Press on a greased baking sheet.

Bake at 350º for 15 minutes or until crisp.

An option is to roll the balls in sugar before pressing onto the baking sheet.

Yields 2 1/2 - 3 dozen

Carol Gotwals

Molasses Crinkles

1 cup brown sugar
3/4 cup shortening
1/4 cup molasses
1 large egg
2 1/4 cups all-purpose flour
2 tsp baking soda
1 tsp ground cinnamon
1 tsp ground ginger
1/2 tsp ground cloves
1/4 tsp salt

Mix brown sugar, shortening, molasses and egg. Mix in flour, baking soda, cinnamon, ginger, cloves and salt. Cover and refrigerate at least one hour.

Preheat oven to 375º.

Shape dough into teaspoonful-size balls. Then dip tops in granulated sugar. Place sugared balls about 3 inches apart on lightly greased cookie sheet.

Bake 10-12 minutes. Immediately remove cookies from sheet with spatula. Cool on rack.

Makes 4 dozen.

Chandler and Nita Barbour

They're just wonderful when warm and you have them with a glass of milk. It was what Aunt Geneva Barbour always had for an afternoon snack.

These are denser when using butter. Nita Barbour always uses the shortening.

Granola Bars

1 stick margarine
1 stick butter
1 cup brown sugar
1 tsp vanilla
2 - 3 eggs (2 if using quick oats)
2 cups (heaping) flour (half white/wheat)
1 tsp baking powder
1 tsp cinnamon
2 cups crispy rice cereal
4 cups oats
1 cup chocolate chips

Preheat oven to 350º.

Melt the butter and margarine. Put in big bowl; add brown sugar, vanilla. Beat in eggs. Add the flour, baking powder and cinnamon. Mix well. Add the rice cereal and oats. It will be a stiff batter. Then fold in the chocolate chips. Spread into 2 greased 9" x 13" pans.

Bake in preheated 350º oven for about 20 - 25 minutes. It's done when the edges are brown.

You could add nuts, seeds, raisins, or wheat germ.

Yields 3 dozen bars

Anne Douglass

"Cutting dessert bars is easier if you score the bars as soon as the pan comes out of the oven. When bars are cool, cut on scored line."

Ginger Crunch Cookies

1 cup sugar
3/4 cup shortening
1 egg
1/4 cup molasses
2 cups flour
2 tsp baking soda
1 tsp cinnamon
1 tsp ginger
1 tsp cloves
1/2 tsp salt

Cream sugar and shortening; add egg and molasses. Stir in dry ingredients; dough should be quite stiff.

Chill dough overnight for best handling.

Roll into walnut-sized balls. Pat down with cold water. Sprinkle with sugar.

Bake at 350º for about 10 minutes.

Yields 2 1/2 dozen cookies

Paula Colwell

Judy Friend's Hermits

3/4 cup melted butter
1 1/2 cups brown sugar
2 eggs
1/4 cup molasses
2 3/4 cups flour
1 tsp each, baking soda, cinnamon, cloves, ginger
1 cup raisins, soaked and drained
1 cup chopped walnuts
Pinch of salt
1/8 cup water
Baking spray for the pan

Preheat oven to 350º.

Combine butter and sugar until fluffy. Beat in 2 eggs. Add molasses and water. Add flour, baking soda, spices, salt and mix well. Add plumped raisins and walnuts.

Spray a 9" x 13" pan with Pam. Spread batter, which will be quite stiff, into pan.

Bake about 20 - 25 minutes. Do not overbake. Center should be a bit "gooey".

Maysie Childs

These keep well and make your house smell wonderful.

Mama's Good Cookies

1 egg
1 cup oil
1 cup butter
2 cups brown sugar
1 tsp vanilla
3 1/2 cups all-purpose flour
1 cup crispy rice cereal
1 cup old fashioned rolled oats
1 cup toasted coconut
1 cup walnuts or pecan pieces

Preheat oven 350º.

Cream the egg, oil, butter, brown sugar and vanilla. Add mixed dry ingredients to the creamed mixture and combine. Spoon as a slightly rounded tablespoonful onto lightly greased or parchment lined baking sheets.

Bake 12 - 15 minutes to desired doneness.

Yields 5 - 6 dozen cookies

Marjorie H Wakefield

"Aunt Marge", my mom, made and used this recipe for the Asthma Camp in Monroe County, PA where it was a real winner. Sometimes she greased two 9" x 13" pans and pressed the dough into the bottoms. She would bake at the same temperature and score to make bars that could be wrapped individually and taken on hikes.

Nancy's Lace Cookies

2 1/4 cups old fashioned, not quick, rolled oats
2 1/4 cups light brown sugar
3 T unbleached flour
1 tsp salt, if butter used is unsalted
1 1/2 cups pecans or walnuts – chopped
1 egg, slightly beaten
1 tsp vanilla extract
3/4 cup melted butter

Heat oven to 375°.

Mix together rolled oats, brown sugar, flour, butter and pecans with spoon. Add egg, vanilla, and melted butter to dry mix and stir with spoon. Drop mixture by leveled tablespoon on greased or un-greased cookie sheet leaving enough room for the cookie to spread out flat. 15 per tray works for me.

Bake in 375° oven for 5 - 7 minutes, until they start to brown around their edges. Wait 2 - 3 minutes to remove from tray with spatula and allow to cool on flat rack. Makes about 4 1/2 dozen cookies.

Note: These are almost impossible to make in the summer, but great in cold weather.

Nancy Hodermarsky

This recipe was given to me by Nell Fallon of Greenfield, Massachusetts. I believe she took it from an oatmeal box.

These wonderful cookies were brought to Rev. Alice Hildebrand's celebration of her island ministry in January 2011. With crunchy pecans and slightly soft inside the crisp edges, they disappeared quickly.

No Bake Chocolate Peanut Butter Bars

2 cups peanut butter (divided use)
3/4 cup butter
2 cups powdered sugar
3 cups graham cracker crumbs
2 cups semi-sweet chocolate chips, divided use

Beat 1 1/4 cups peanut butter and butter until creamy. Gradually beat in 1 cup powdered sugar. With hand or wooden spoon, work in remaining powdered sugar, graham cracker crumbs and 1/2 cup chocolate chips. Press evenly into 9" x 13" pan. Smooth top.

Melt remaining peanut butter and 1 1/2 cup chocolate chips in heavy duty pan, over lowest heat. Stir constantly until smooth. (Note: or you could carefully melt and mix the combination in a microwave for 30 seconds, stirring and reheating until smooth). Spread over crumb mixture. Chill one hour or until the chocolate is firm.

Cut into as many bars as you wish.

Dottie Bonnet

Orange Chocolate Chip Cookies

1 lb butter
1 cup granulated sugar
1 cup brown sugar
1 1/2 T orange zest
2 T orange juice, from zested orange
2 eggs
1 1/2 T orange extract
5 cups flour
1/2 tsp baking soda
1 cup chocolate chips
1 1/2 tsp salt

Heat oven to 350º.

Cream butter and sugars. Add eggs, zest, juice and orange extract and beat well. Mix flour, salt, and soda together. Add dry ingredients to moist mixture. Beat until just mixed. Add chips and gently stir in.

Prepare baking pans with cooking spray, parchment paper or silicone baking sheet.

Drop from any size table or soupspoon desired, or a #20 (3 1/2 T) portion scoop for largest cookies. They don't spread too much.

Bake about 20 minutes or until lightly browned.

Yields 5 - 6 dozen small cookies

Joleen Dodge

I wanted to have the orange and chocolate flavors together in a soft cookie. This resulted in my creating this cookie while baking for a local island restaurant.

Fruit-Oatmeal Bars*

1 cup quick-cooking rolled oats
1/2 cup all-purpose white flour
1/2 cup whole wheat pastry flour
2/3 cup packed light brown sugar
1/4 tsp baking soda
1/4 cup canola oil
3 T apple or cranberry juice
1 cup fruit preserves
1/4 tsp salt
Cooking spray

Preheat oven to 325º.

Coat an 8" x 12" inch baking dish with nonstick cooking spray; set aside.

Combine oats, flour, brown sugar, salt and baking soda in a large bowl until no lumps of brown sugar remain. Drizzle oil and fruit juice over the oats and mix until evenly moistened and crumbly.

Set aside 1/2 cup of mixture for the topping; press the remainder evenly in the bottom of the baking dish. Spread preserves over the top. Sprinkle with the reserved topping.

Bake until golden, about 30 - 40 minutes. Let cool in the baking dish on a rack. Cut into 15 bars. Store at room temperature in an airtight container.

Yields 15 bars

Eliza Spencer

* Courtesy of Move It To Lose It

Simple Cookies

Graham Crackers
1 cup sugar
1 cup butter
1 cup chopped pecans

Set oven at 350°. Select cookie sheet with sides.

Put graham crackers on cookie sheet, lined up in rows. Put butter and sugar in saucepan. Bring to boil and boil for 2 minutes or until frothy. Spread butter and sugar mixture on top of cookies. Sprinkle with chopped pecans. Bake for ten minutes.

Cut along graham cracker lines while hot. Leave in pan until cool.

Lola Marston

"Some holiday cookies require an indent on top to fill with jam or chocolate. Use a honey dipper rounded end to make the indentation."

Mar's Lemon Squares

Crust:
1 cup flour
1/2 cup butter
1/4 cup confectioners sugar

Filling:
2 eggs
1 cup sugar
1 T flour
1/2 tsp baking powder
2 T lemon juice
2 T grated lemon rind

Preheat oven 325°.

Mix like a pie crust to just stick together. Bake 15 minutes in a greased 8" square pan.

Mix filling and pour over crust. Return to oven and bake 20 minutes still at 325°.

Sometimes I sprinkle with confectioners sugar just before serving. Cut while warm into 2" squares.

Serves 16

Marjory Chesney

I like that my grandchildren and other family members have favorite recipes that they like me to make. These are the favorite of grandson Eric.

They are always a big hit at the Sunbeam Fair that the mostly longtime Sunset summer residents, especially the children, have put on each summer for many years. The fair supports the Sunbeam and helps the social mission of the members of the vessel to the Maine islanders.

Mincemeat Squares

1 1/2 cups unbleached flour
1/2 tsp baking powder
1/2 tsp salt
3/4 cup butter
1 cup brown sugar
1 1/2 cups rolled oats or granola
Pint mincemeat or other thick jam

Preheat oven to 350°.

Combine all but mincemeat or jam to make a crumble mixture. Layer in greased 9" x 13" baking pan: Use 1/2 of the crumble mixture on the bottom, dot and spread with all of the mincemeat or thick jam, and top with the remaining crumble mixture. Bake for about 30 - 40 minutes or until top is lightly browned. Cool in pan on wire rack and cut into squares or strips.

Serves 18

Note: Other fillings can be used.

Charlotte Davis

This recipe was a gift from Marge Judkins, a former neighbor and friend in South Deer Isle. I've made it with Gwen's green tomato mincemeat, Sue Wyard's kid mincemeat and from venison mincemeat---all gifts from other neighbors or family. Minces all contain dried fruits, candied peels, cinnamon, nutmeg, cloves and often nuts. I usually prefer them in this oatmeal-like bar.

Saucy Bars

1/2 cup butter
1 cup white sugar
1 cup hot apple sauce
2 cups flour
1 tsp baking soda
1/2 tsp salt
1/2 tsp cloves
1 tsp cinnamon
1 tsp nutmeg
1 cup raisins
1/2 cup walnuts, chopped
1 tsp vanilla extract

Icing:
2 T milk
2 cups confectioners sugar
1 tsp vanilla extract
Dash salt

Preheat oven 350°.

Cream butter and sugar. Mix in applesauce. Add remainder of ingredients and mix together until smooth.

Spread evenly in greased 9" x 13" pan. Bake for 25 minutes at 350°.

Combine icing and stir until smooth. Ice bars while still warm.

Makes 16 - 20 bars

Jan Rosati

Adapted from Lloyd Capen's, Deer Isle, Maine recipe. He and his wife Marge, another quilter, were famous for their Highmeadow Farm with fresh pressed cider and fresh and canned fruits and jams.

Pumpkin Chocolate Chip Cookies

1 1/2 cups of canned pumpkin (from a 15 oz can)
1 1/2 cups white sugar
3/4 cup vegetable oil
1 1/2 T milk
1 egg beaten
3 cups all-purpose flour
3 tsp baking powder
1 1/2 tsp cinnamon
1 1/2 tsp baking soda
1 1/2 tsp vanilla
1 1/2 cups chocolate chips
3/4 cup nuts, broken
3/4 tsp salt

Preheat oven to 375º.

Beat eggs; add sugar and cream well until blended. Add oil and canned pumpkin, stirring to combine. Sift flour, baking powder, baking soda, salt and cinnamon. Add dry ingredients to wet pumpkin mixture and stir. Add milk and vanilla. Stir to incorporate. Then, stir in chocolate chips and broken nuts to finish.

Drop by rounded tablespoons onto an ungreased baking or cookie sheet. Bake 9 - 11 minutes.

Yields 2 1/2 - 3 dozen cookies

Susan Perez

I usually bake these as a bar by spreading dough into a greased 13" x 9" baking pan. I bake the bars 12 - 15 minutes and cool them in the pan I can vary the serving size by the crowd and the way I cut the bars in the pan.

Ruby's Split-Second Shortbread

3/4 cup soft butter
2/3 cup sugar
1 egg
2 cups flour
1/2 tsp baking powder
2 tsp vanilla
Jam or jelly of choice

Preheat oven to 350º.

Cream together butter and sugar; beat in the egg and vanilla. Combine flour and baking powder. Add to the above mixture to have a stiff batter.

Form 2 loaves, like French bread, on ungreased baking sheet. With your finger make a shallow trench lengthwise through the center of each loaf. Fill with jam or jelly of your choice.

Bake 20 minutes until golden. Cool 5 minutes and then cut on diagonal.

Yields 2 loaves

Lanny Anderson

This is an easy peasy recipe that even the guys in the family like to bake. I like it because it is good and it uses up scraps of those nice jams.

Choir led by music director Win Pusey, flowers by Eliza Spencer, reading by Chandler Barbour and Richard Howe

Bill Anderson icing a cake

Chapter 7

Isaiah 55:2

Why do you spend your money for that which is not bread, and your labor for that which does not satisfy? Listen diligently to me, and eat what is good, and delight yourselves in rich food.

Allie's Mincemeat Pie

2 lbs lean chopped (not ground) beef
1 lb beef suet, finely chopped
5 lbs apples, peeled and diced
2 lbs whole raisins
2 lbs currants
1 T cloves
1 T nutmeg
1 T cinnamon
1 quart cider
1 pint molasses (not blackstrap)
1 T salt

Hard Sauce
1 1/2 cups powdered sugar
3/4 cup unsalted butter
1 pint good brandy

Blend ingredients in blender.

Bring all ingredients except brandy to a boil and simmer slowly for 1 1/2 hours. Add brandy. This can be frozen or placed in sterilized preserving jars. The jars should be put in a hot water bath with water 1" above the jars and processed for 1 1/2 hours.

For mincemeat pies, double a regular pie crust recipe. Make 2 rectangular sheets of dough and freeze for 10 minutes. Put cooled butter in one, fold and roll the dough slightly. Fold again with butter in another fold, roll slightly and put in freezer for 10 more minutes. Repeat again, and again. Roll half dough, putting it in a glass pie mold. Refrigerate bottom while rolling the top. Roll the dough for top and cut with cookie cutters—hearts, diamonds, etc. to make overlapping pattern on top of the pie.

When making pies, create more texture by adding to one jar of mincemeat 2 - 3 Granny Smith apples, diced to 1/4", 1/2 cup raisins, some currants, the juice of 1 lemon and 4 T brandy.

Bake for 30 minutes at 375°.

Kenna Haines

This recipe is from my Swedish greatgrandmother, Albertine Wendel Grace from Arlee, Montana. It was a recipe given to her by the Scottish mother of Albertine's second husband.

Swedish Almond Cake

25 sweet almonds, peeled (1.5 oz)
1/2 tsp Swedish almond extract or 6 bitter almonds
1 egg
1 1/3 cups sugar
2/3 cup milk
1 1/3 cups flour
1/2 tsp baking powder
1 T vanilla sugar
2/3 cup melted and cooled butter

Heat oven to 390°. Prepare the 9" pan by coating it with shortening and flouring it.

Melt the butter and cool. Grind almonds in a food processor and remove.

In the food processor, whisk the sugar and egg until light and fluffy. Add the ground almonds and extract with the milk to the egg sugar mixture in the processor.

In a bowl, sift together the flour, vanilla sugar and baking powder. Add the flour mixture a little at a time to the ingredients in the processor and blend. Add the melted butter last.

Pour into 9" cake pan and bake for 30 minutes or until the center springs back to your touch.

When it has cooled completely, frost with powdered sugar mixed with either cream, milk and almond extract, or a little lemon juice and milk.

Kenna Haines

This recipe is from our friend and Swedish teacher, Annette Johansson Los.

Angel Pie

6 egg whites
1/4 tsp cream of tartar
1 cup sugar
3/4 tsp vanilla extract
1/4 tsp salt
Bitter chocolate for topping (optional)

Butter a 9" pie pan. Preheat oven to 275°.

Beat egg whites, salt and cream of tartar until stiff.

A spoonful at a time, beat in sugar and then add vanilla. Spread the above combined mixture into the pan, heaping the edge higher to make a rim. Bake until dry and firm to the touch, but not brown, about 1 hour.

Turn off heat and cool in oven with door open. Let stand several hours or overnight in the refrigerator. If using filling, add at this point. Spread with 1 1/2 cups cream, whipped but not sweetened. Shave bitter chocolate over top, if desired.

Lemon Filling Version:
4 egg yolks
1/4 cup sugar
1/4 cup lemon juice

Beat 4 egg yolks until thick with 1/4 cup sugar and 1/4 cup lemon juice. Cook over hot water until thick and smooth. Cool. Add where indicated above.

Serves 6 - 8

Dee Miller

Any church cookbook should have at least one "angelic" recipe!

Black Midnight Cake

2/3 cup shortening
1 2/3 cups sugar
3 eggs
2 1/4 cups flour
2/3 cup cocoa
1/4 tsp baking powder
1/4 tsp soda
1 tsp vanilla
1 tsp salt

Heat oven to 350.

Cream shortening, sugar and eggs. Sift together the dry ingredients and mix them in alternately with 1 1/3 cups water and vanilla mixture.

Pour into 2 8" greased pans for a layer cake, or a Bundt pan.

Bake at 350° for 40-50 minutes.

For frosting, I use a prepared frosting and whip it.

Yields 12 - 15 servings

Eliza Spencer

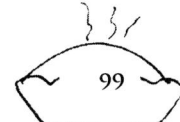

Boiled Raisin Fruit Cake

2 cups raisins
1 1/2 cups sugar
1/2 cup margarine
2 eggs
3 cups flour
2 tsp soda
1 tsp nutmeg
1 tsp ground cloves
1 tsp cinnamon
2 cups candied fruit
1 cup nuts, to taste
1 tsp salt

Heat oven to 350º.

Boil raisins in water to cover. Reserve one cup of this water and cool. Cream together sugar, margarine and eggs. Mix together dry ingredients. Add dry mix to creamed mixture and add 1 cup of raisin water and mix. Add raisins, candied fruit and nuts. Fill 2 greased and floured bread pans about 1/2 full. Can also top with a few nuts.

Bake for one hour at 350º.

Yields 2 loaves

Margie Nevells

I got this recipe for fruitcake from Barbara Nevells, who got it from her sister-in-law, Letha Bray. It's very good and easy. It should be made a month or two before you want to serve it. This also freezes very well.

Bon Temps New Orleans Bread Pudding

3 T butter
1 loaf French bread, cut in cubes
1 quart milk
3 eggs
2 cups sugar
2 tsp vanilla
1 cup raisins

Sauce:
1/2 cup butter
1 cup sugar
1 egg
1 - 2 jiggers* of whiskey

Heat oven to 350º.

Melt butter in bottom of 9" x 13" baking dish. Place bread cubes in baking dish and pour milk over it to soak. Beat eggs, sugar, vanilla; add raisins. Pour egg mixture over bread in baking dish.

Bake at 350º until firm, about 45 minutes.

Sauce: Cook sugar and butter in double boiler until sugar has dissolved. Add beaten egg and whiskey.

Pour over pudding, then broil until slightly brown. Watch carefully.

Serves 12

*1 jigger = about 1 1/2 fluid oz

Emily Wiegand

Cherry Cream Cheese Pie

4 cups fresh cherries
1 1/3 cups sugar
1/3 cup flour
3/4 tsp almond extract
8 oz cream cheese
1 egg
1/2 cup sugar
2 1/2 cups flour
1 cup lard
1 egg
1 tsp salt

Heat oven to 425°.

Mix sugar and flour together; stir lightly with cherries that have been washed, drained and pitted. Sprinkle extract on top. Set aside.

Beat cream cheese, egg and 1/2 cup sugar together until light and fluffy. Set aside.

For crust, mix flour, salt and lard well in large bowl. Put 1 egg, lightly beaten, in a cup and fill with water to make 1/2 cup. Add to flour bowl; mix and roll out. In 8-inch pie plate, place bottom crust. Add cherry mixture. Then top with cream cheese mixture. Cover with top crust; slit, seal and flute.

Bake at 425° for 30 minutes or until crust is nicely browned. Serve warm.

Yields 1 8" pie

Helen McKinnon

Served warm at Sunset Church coffee hour September 2010 and quickly enjoyed by many.

Chocolate Coffee Rum Cake

3 cups flour
1 1/2 tsp baking soda
12 oz pkg semi-sweet chocolate chips
3 sticks unsalted butter, cut into pieces
1/3 cup dark rum
2 cups strong brewed coffee
2 1/4 cups sugar
3 large eggs, lightly beaten
1 1/2 tsp vanilla extract
Powdered sugar for dusting
1/4 tsp salt

Heat oven to 300°.

Grease and generously flour a 4 1/2" deep 12 cup Bundt pan.

Combine flour, baking soda and salt.

In a double boiler, melt chocolate and butter slowly stirring until smooth. Remove chocolate from heat and place in a large mixing bowl. Stir in rum, coffee and sugar. Beat in flour mixture, 1/2 cup at a time, scraping down sides of bowl. Add eggs and vanilla until batter is well combined. Pour batter into prepared pan. Bake cake on middle shelf of the oven about 1 hour and 50 minutes until tester comes out clean. Let cake cool completely in pan on a rack, then turn it out onto a plate.

Dust cake with powdered sugar and serve with halved strawberries, raspberries, or vanilla ice cream.

Yields 12 - 16 servings

Can be made 3 days in advance. Wrap well and chill to keep even longer.

Carolyn Eberdt

This is very, very moist! Absolutely fabulous!

Cold Lemon Soufflé

1 T gelatin (one envelope)
3 eggs, separated
1 cup sugar
1 tsp vanilla
1/3 cup lemon juice
1 lemon zest
2 cups heavy cream
1/4 cup cold water

Soak gelatin in cold water. It will become opaque and firm. In order to use gelatin, it must be heated after soaking. Place container of soaked gelatin in pan of hot water and heat until it becomes clear and liquid. It is then ready to mix with the other ingredients.

Beat yolks until pale and lemon-colored. Add sugar gradually and beat until very light. Beat in juice, grated lemon zest and vanilla. Add the gelatin.

Allow mixture to cool until starting to congeal. Now fold in the stiffly beaten cream, then the stiffly beaten egg whites.

Put mixture into a serving bowl or soufflé dish and chill several hours. Do not freeze.

Serves 8

Martha Massey

Cracker Pie and Strawberries

3 egg whites
1/4 tsp cream of tartar
1 cup white sugar
1 cup chopped walnuts
1 tsp vanilla
1 tsp baking powder
12 crushed salted square crackers
1 quart fresh or 2 pounds frozen strawberries
1 cup cream, whipped

Heat oven to 325°.

In a large bowl, beat egg whites to froth. Add cream of tartar, and continue beating until egg whites form stiff peaks. Gradually add the sugar into the egg whites. Gently fold in the nuts, vanilla, baking powder, and crushed crackers.

Place in a greased 9" pie plate. Bake at 325° for 30 minutes. Turn off oven and let sit in oven with door ajar for 1 - 2 hours.

Serve with strawberries and whipped cream.

Serves 8 - 10

Recipe can easily be doubled: use a 9" x 13" or 8" x 14" baking dish, 2 quarts strawberries (or 4 1 lb pkg frozen berries), 2 cups whipped cream.

Serves 16 - 20.

Ann Hooke

Danish Ris A' La Manda Dessert

1 cup rice
4 cups milk
8 T sugar
2 envelopes gelatin
2 cups whipped cream
2 tsp vanilla extract
1/2 tsp salt

In a medium-sized, heavy bottomed saucepan, bring the rice, milk and salt to a boil over high heat. Reduce heat to low and simmer until the rice is tender (about 20 - 25 minutes). Be mindful and stir frequently so that rice does not stick and scorch.

Add sugar and gelatin that has been dissolved in a little cold water for 3 - 5 minutes to moisten and avoid clumping, as per gelatin packages.

Cool and then add whipped cream and vanilla and nutmeg, if using.

Put in a bowl and chill until ready to serve, which will help it to maintain its thickened state.

Serves 8

Ingeborg Hansen

At Christmas dinner we place one whole almond in the bowl of pudding. The finder of the almond wins a marzipan pig!

Island Miracle Cake

1 lemon cake mix
12 oz can of lemon-lime soda

Preheat over to 350°.

Grease and dust pans with a little flour. Combine mix and soda. Bake in prepared pans at 350° until done.

To keep it vegan, frost with a spreadable mixture of lemon juice and confectioners sugar.

Serves 8 - 10

Peter Elliott

Trust a young bachelor to come up with this fantastic cake. He says it is very versatile. You can use a chocolate or vanilla cake with crème soda, and an orange cake with orange soda.

"When grating citrus peel, bits of peel are often stuck in the holes of the grater. Rather than waste the peel (with all that flavor), you can brush it off with a clean toothbrush."

Lily Pond Chocolate Pudding

3/4 cup sugar
1 cup flour
2 tsp baking powder
1/8 tsp salt
2 T butter
1 oz unsweetened baking chocolate (or 3 T cocoa powder)
1/2 cup milk
2 tsp vanilla extract

Topping:
1/4 cup sugar
1/2 cup brown sugar
4 T powdered cocoa
1 cup cold water or coffee

Heat oven to 350°.

Sift the dry ingredients. Melt together over hot water (in double boiler) the butter and chocolate. When melted and stirred together, add this mixture to the flour mixture; stir in milk and vanilla. Mix as little as possible until fully blended.

Pour into a buttered baking dish (roughly 9" x 9" inches or equivalent).

Combine the white and brown sugars and the cocoa and scatter over the top without stirring.

Pour over the top the cold water or coffee.

Bake 40 minutes at 350°.

Allen Myers

Joy's Easy Chocolate Mousse Pie

Graham cracker crust
6 oz dark chocolate bar (at least 65% chocolate)
10 oz Cool Whip

Prepare graham cracker crust.

Melt broken pieces of chocolate carefully over hot water or in microwave. Let cool until room temperature. Fold in Cool Whip. Pour into pie crust and refrigerate until serving.

Garnish pie with chocolate bar curls from any of the chocolate bar that is left.

Serves 8

Joy Kyper

"Professionally decorated cakes have a silky, molten look. To get that appearance, frost your cake as usual, then use a hair dryer to blow dry the surface until the frosting slightly melts."

Chocolate Erotica

1 chocolate cake mix
1 box instant chocolate pudding
1 pkg chocolate chips
1 3/4 cup milk

Heat oven to 350º.

Mix ingredients well. Pour into greased and floured tunnel or bundt pan. Bake until done, about 45 minutes.

I don't frost this because it's so rich. Dust with confectioners sugar or serve with whipped cream.

Eliza Spencer

"To ensure you have equal amounts of batter in each pan when making layered cake, use a kitchen scale to measure the weight."

Fresh Maine Blueberry Pie

1 quart Maine blueberries (save 1 cup for later)
1 cup sugar
3/4 cup water
2 T cornstarch
1/4 tsp salt

Heat oven to 375º.

Roll out pie dough to fit bottom of 9 or 10 inch pie plate. Bake in 375º oven until done (light to medium brown). Cool thoroughly.

Mix cornstarch, salt and 1/4 cup water until cornstarch dissolves. Add to 1 cup Maine blueberries, 1 cup (or less) sugar, 1/2 cup remaining water. Cook on stove until mixture boils up into clear dark blue thick mixture. Cool.

When cool, add to 3 cups cold blueberries for 9" pie, to 4 cups cold blueberries for 10" pie. Pour into cooled crust and refrigerate.

Yields 1 9" or 10" pie

Nancy Hodermarsky

The blueberries must be small wild berries of Maine or New Hampshire. Big commercial berries will not gel. I often add a few red raspberries or peaches to the mixture at the end.

I received this recipe from my neighbor, Annie Pressey.

Frozen Yogurt Pie for Marthas

16 oz any flavor fruit yogurt
8 oz tub of frozen whipped topping
Fresh or frozen berries
1 10" graham cracker pie crust

Thaw the frozen whipped topping enough to stir it with yogurt and berries. Pour the mixture into the piecrust and freeze at least 4 hours. To serve, thaw about 1/2 hour to allow ease of cutting while still remaining frozen.

Serves 6

Susan E (Harris) Seater

Recipes from my mother, Ruth E. Harris (1924-2005). She served this dessert annually when the Sunset Ladies Aid met at her barn for the Fir Bag Stuffing Party before the Summer Fair. The recipe came from her NJ neighbor, Dora Mullins.

The Aid was a descendant of the Marthas, the Sunset women of the Martha Washington Benevolent Society (1836-1943). Naomi (Warren) Eaton who lived in our house until 1906 was a secretary for the Marthas and treasurer for the Hillside Cemetery, started by the Marthas in 1861. Naomi may have used our 1840 barn for the same purpose. Ruth was an officer of the Aid and the Cemetery and the Sunset Church. Her grandmother was a charter member of the Aid.

Sylvesters' Spiced Peaches

29 oz can peach halves
1/2 cup vinegar
1/2 cup sugar
1 whole stick cinnamon
1/2 tsp whole cloves

Two days before serving drain 29 oz can peach halves, reserving 1 cup syrup.

For syrup, in a small sauce pan combine cup syrup, vinegar, sugar, cinnamon and cloves. Simmer uncovered for 5-10 minutes. Add peach halves studded with whole cloves. Bring to a boil; cool and refrigerate at least 2 days in a tight container.

To serve, drain and heap in serving dish.

May use 2 cans of pear halves or 2 cans of pineapple spears in place of peaches.

Serves 6

Norma Sheard

"The smell of good bread baking, like the sound of lightly flowing water, is indescribable in its evocation of innocence and delight."

M.F.K. Fisher

Fruit Cake à la Alice and Allen

1 pound pitted dates, chopped coarsely
1 cup walnuts, coarsely chopped
1 cup raisins
1 package candied cherries
1 package candied pineapple chunks
1/2 pound flaked coconut
14 oz can sweetened condensed milk

Put a pan of hot water on a lower shelf in the oven and preheat to 300º. Prepare all fruit and nuts with a coarse cut and place in a bowl. Add coconut last and mix well, with hands in sprayed plastic sandwich bags. Stir in sweetened condensed milk. Blend well. Grease and line the 6" x 3" x 2" pan with greased paper bag cut to size. Pack firmly into pan. Bake for 1 1/2 hours, at preheated temperature, over the steaming water. Remove from oven. Run knife/spatula around pan rim. When barely warm, take paper off cake. Keeps indefinitely in tight tin cans.

Serves 16

If you double the recipe it is just right for a 10" tube pan. Otherwise a 6 X 3 X 2 inch (bread) pan is appropriate, if properly greased and lined with greased butcher's/parchment or brown paper.

Options: If doubling recipe, you can add other candied fruits: currants, citron, candied lemon or orange rinds, apricots, raisins (jumbo preferred) and/or other nuts: pecans, brazil nuts, blanched almonds and 3 T of flour.

Charlo Davis

This remarkable cake was served on Saint Nicholas Day, 2004 at Alice and Allen's Open House at the parsonage, Deer Isle, ME. It was served with Brandy-less Dried Fruit and Nuts Balls, 2 Cheese Balls and Crackers, Carrot Sticks, No Bake cookies, Roasted Nuts, Grapes, Powdered sugar cookies, Cold red punch and Decaf. The creche, on table, had numerous mini animals and personages. The tree had Alice's German father's decorations. Her mother, with her Quaker beliefs, did not celebrate Christmas. However, the fruit cake was Alice's mother's, with no flour or liquor, that Allen baked that time.

Grandmother's Old English Plum Pudding

1 lb blanched split or ground almonds
2 lbs dark raisins
2 lbs currants
1/2 lb chopped citron peel

Sift and add to above:
1 lb unbleached flour (about 3 cups)
1/2 tsp ground cloves
1/2 tsp nutmeg
1 tsp cinnamon
Pinch of mace

Beat until fluffy:
10 extra large eggs
Add: 1 lb sugar
Add: 1 lb melted butter
Add 1 cup brandy if desired

Pour into well-greased pudding molds with lids; steam for about 3 hours on a rack in closed pan. When pudding has cooled somewhat, remove from mold and finish cooling. Wrap well in cheesecloth and foil. Store in a cool place and allow to mellow. Remove foil occasionally and give pudding a brandy drink right through the cheese cloth. Rewrap and continue aging until Christmas.

To serve, remove cheese cloth and wrap in foil. Put in 300º oven and warm through about 20 - 30 minutes. Pour hot brandy over pudding on ceramic plate and light with a match as you bring to table.

Serve with creamy sauce below:
Beat 1 egg until foamy. Blend in 1/3 cup of butter (melted), 1 1/2 cups sifted confectioners sugar and 1 tsp vanilla. Fold in 1 cup of whipping cream, whipped stiff. Makes 2 1/2 cups.

Norma V. Sheard

Election Day is a good time to prepare Grandmother's pudding for Christmas!

Cutter Key Lime Pie

6 oz cream cheese
1 can sweetened condensed milk
4 oz Cool Whip
1/4 cup sour cream
1/2 cup key lime juice (important to use key lime)

Whip cream cheese until smooth. Add condensed milk. Fold in sour cream, whipped topping and key lime juice. Pour into graham cracker shell.

Refrigerate at least two hours before serving.

Makes one 8" or 9" pie.

Suzanne Sonneborn

I usually freeze it and remove it at the beginning of a meal; in 30 minutes it can be cut and served. Easy, tasty, refreshing dessert that can be made ahead and kept on hand for guests.

I take great liberties with this recipe and use all non-fat or low fat ingredients, often put in the whole 8 oz package of cream cheese, and also increase the whipped topping. No matter how I adapt it, it's always good!

Buoy Blueberry Cake

1 1/2 cups sifted flour
3/4 cup sugar
2 tsp baking powder
1/2 tsp salt
1/4 cup butter
1 egg
1/2 cup milk (or a little more)
1 cup fresh blueberries

Heat oven to 350º.

Sift dry ingredients together, add milk, egg, butter and then fold in blueberries. Put into a greased 8" x 10" pan. Sprinkle the top with cinnamon sugar. Bake at 350º for 25 to 30 minutes

Lemon Sauce:
1/2 cup sugar
1 T cornstarch
1 cup water
1/4 cup fresh squeezed lemon juice
1 tsp butter
Grated nutmeg

Mix sugar and cornstarch. Add water and bring to a slow boil. Stir until thick and creamy. Add lemon juice and butter. Grate nutmeg over the sauce. Spoon hot lemon sauce over each serving of cake.

Will also make great blueberry muffins if put into muffin tins and baked at 400º for about 20 minutes. Leave off cinnamon topping for muffins.

Judith Knight McMillan

This is my great grandmother's recipe found by my mother, Rusty Knight, in Levi Knight's farm house on the Reach Road. The house is no longer there as it burned in a fire back in the late 1970s or early 1980s.

Maine Blueberry Cake

1 1/4 cup Maine blueberries
1 T flour
3/4 cup sugar
1/2 stick butter or margarine
2 eggs
1/2 cup milk
2 cups sifted flour
2 tsp baking powder
1/8 cup sugar
1/8 tsp nutmeg or cinnamon
1 T lemon zest (optional)

Heat oven to 350º.

Mix blueberries with 1 tablespoon flour so berries do not stick together. Cream together sugar and butter. Add eggs and beat until light and add milk. Sift 2 cups flour. Sift again with 2 tsp baking powder. Combine flour with eggs, butter, sugar and berries above. Spread mixture evenly in pan. Add lemon zest if desired.

Top with sugar mixed with nutmeg or cinnamon.

Grease 9" x 13" x 2" inch pan. and bake 35 minutes until done (test with toothpick).

Serves 12 - 15

Rosemary Stoller

Mrs. Wood's Pound Cake

2 cups flour
2 tsp baking powder
1/2 tsp salt
1/2 cup milk
1 tsp vanilla extract
8 T butter
8 T shortening or margarine
4 eggs
1 1/2 cups sugar

Heat oven to 350º.

Mix flour, baking powder, salt, milk, vanilla, butter, shortening, eggs and sugar together in an electric mixer for 20 minutes.

Bake in a greased 9" tube pan for 1 hour.

Serves 12

Carol Gotwals

This cake has lots of uses from short cake with fruit or by itself without icing. It is one of my favorite recipes.

Pots de Crème

12 oz bag semi-sweet chocolate chips
1/2 tsp vanilla
2 eggs
1 1/2 cup milk or 1 cup cream and 1/2 cup milk, scalded
2 pinches salt

Mix together chocolate chips, vanilla, eggs, milk and salt into blender.

Pour mixture into wine glasses or little demitasse cups, leaving plenty of room to add a heap of whipped cream later for garnish. Place in refrigerator for at least 3 - 4 hours so mixture will set.

Alternative recipe:
Use strong hot coffee instead of milk and cream, 12 oz of semi-sweet chocolate chips, 4 whole eggs at room temperature, 2 tsp vanilla extract or liqueur. Place chocolate chips in blender, topped by eggs and the vanilla extract (or liqueur). Add a pinch of salt. Turn on blender. While it is blending, remove circular disk from the blender lid, and very slowly pour in 8 oz of strong, very hot coffee. This is essential.

Serves 6 - 8

Alice Hildebrand

Pumpkin Pudding

2 cups roasted pumpkin (or one 15 oz can pumpkin)
1 can evaporated milk
2 eggs, beaten
1/2 cup brown sugar
1/2 tsp ginger
1/4 tsp nutmeg
1/8 tsp cloves
1 tsp cinnamon
1/8 tsp black pepper
1/2 tsp salt

Topping
1/2 cup brown sugar
1 cup coarse (cubed and dry) bread crumbs
1/2 cup slivered almonds (or chopped walnuts)
1 tsp coriander
1/4 tsp cloves
1/2 tsp nutmeg
1 tsp cinnamon
2 T olive oil (not extra-virgin)

Heat oven to 400°.

Cut pumpkin in half. Remove seeds. Coat lightly with olive oil. Bake cut side down on cookie sheet at 400° for about an hour or until soft. Cool. Remove skin and mash in large bowl. Add evaporated milk and beaten eggs. Stir well. Add brown sugar, salt, ginger, nutmeg, cloves, cinnamon and black pepper. Place in lightly oiled deep, baking dish. Bake uncovered at 425° for 15 minutes. Bake an additional 15 minutes at 350°.

Prepare topping.
Combine dry ingredients (brown sugar, bread crumbs, almonds, coriander, cloves, nutmeg, and cinnamon). Add the olive oil gradually and toss crumb mixture lightly. Place topping on pudding. Bake 20 minutes longer at 350°.

Serves 6 - 8

Ann Hooke

Raspberry Walnut Torte

1 1/4 cups flour
1/3 cup powdered sugar
1/2 cup soft butter
20 oz frozen raspberries, thawed
3/4 cup walnuts
2 eggs
1 cup sugar
1/2 tsp baking powder
1 tsp vanilla extract
Whipped cream
1/2 tsp salt

Raspberry Sauce:
1/2 cup water
1/2 cup sugar
2 T cornstarch

Heat oven to 350º.

Combine 1 cup flour, powdered sugar and butter. Blend well. Press mixture into bottom of 13" x 9" pan. Bake for 15 minutes. Let cool.

Drain raspberries; reserve half of liquid for sauce. Spoon berries over crust. Sprinkle with walnuts.

Beat eggs with sugar until light and fluffy. Add salt, 1/4 cup flour, baking powder and vanilla. Blend well. Pour over walnuts. Bake at 350º for 30-35 minutes. Cool. Cut into squares.

Serve with whipped cream and sauce.

Raspberry Sauce: Combine water, sugar, cornstarch and reserved raspberry liquid. Cook until thick.

Serves 12 - 15

Gail Sytsema

Rhubarb Cake

1 1/2 cups sugar
1/2 cup shortening
1 egg
1 cup sour milk
1 tsp vanilla extract
1 T baking soda
2 cups flour
1 1/2 cups diced rhubarb
1/2 tsp salt

Topping:
1/2 cup sugar
1 tsp cinnamon
1/4 cup nuts

Heat oven to 350º.

Mix together shortening, sugar and egg,; then add vanilla.

Sift dry ingredients and add to shortening mixture with sour milk. Fold in rhubarb. Pour into a well greased and floured 9" x 13" pan.

For the topping, combine sugar, cinnamon and nuts. Sprinkle over top of batter.

Bake at 350º for 30 minutes.

This makes a large cake and is especially good when served warm.

Serves 15 - 20

Marjory Chesney & Maurine Tobin

Rum Cake

1 yellow cake mix
1 vanilla instant pudding mix
3 eggs
1/2 cup oil
1/2 cup water
1/2 cup rum
1 cup finely chopped walnuts or pecans

Glaze:
1 stick butter
1/4 cup water
1 cup sugar
1/2 cup rum

Preheat oven to 325°.

Grease and flour bundt or tube cake pan and sprinkle with chopped nuts.

Combine cake mix, pudding mix, eggs, oil, water and rum in large bowl. Mix for 2 minutes on medium speed. Pour in cake pan and bake for 50 minutes.

Let cool for 15 minutes while preparing glaze.

Melt butter, sugar and water and boil for 5 minutes. Remove from heat and add rum. Remove cake from baking pan and drizzle glaze over the cake while warm.

Yields 12 servings

Jeannie Malone

Zucchini Pineapple Cake

2 eggs
2 cups sugar
1 cup vegetable oil
2 tsp vanilla extract
2 tsp cinnamon
2 tsp baking powder
1 tsp baking soda
1 tsp salt
3 cups all-purpose flour
8 oz can crushed pineapple, drained well
1 cup chopped pecans or walnuts
1/2 cup raisins
1/2 cup grated carrots
2 cups grated raw unpeeled zucchini

Preheat oven to 350°.

Beat eggs and sugar together. Add oil and vanilla and beat well. Combine cinnamon, baking powder, baking soda, salt and flour together and add to above. Drain the pineapple, squeeze the zucchini in a towel, grate the carrots and chop the nuts. When ready, stir fruit, veggies and nuts into the batter.

Pour mixture into a 10" greased and floured, tube pan. Bake 350° for about 1 1/3 hours. Cool. Take cake out of the Bundt pan and drizzle with the glaze which is a mixture of 1 cup confectioners sugar and 1-3 T milk.

Sometimes I use a cream cheese frosting.

Serves 10 - 12

Holly Meade

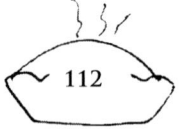

Bell Buoy Fruit Torte

1 pint plums
3/4 cup sugar
1/2 cup butter
1 cup sifted flour
1 tsp baking powder
2 eggs
Dash of salt
Lemon juice
Cinnamon

Cream sugar and butter. Add flour, baking powder, salt and eggs. Place in 9" springform pan. Cover top with fruit.

Sprinkle top with sugar, lemon juice and cinnamon to taste.

Bake one hour at 350°.

Serves 6

Fran Hotchkiss

"Be the change that you wish to see in the world."

Mahatma Gandhi

Rhubarb Crisp

Filling:
2 cups fresh rhubarb, thinly sliced
1 cup mandarin oranges (drained)
1 cup crushed pineapple (drained)
1 cup white sugar
1/4 cup white flour
1 orange peel, zested

Crisp:
1/2 cup brown sugar
1/2 cup dry oatmeal
1/2 cup chopped walnuts
1/2 cup white flour
1/4 cup olive oil

Heat oven to 400°.

Combine the rhubarb, mandarin oranges, pineapple. Combine sugar, flour, and orange zest. Stir into fruit mixture. Place fruit mixture in 8" x 8" baking dish.

To make crisp: combine brown sugar, dry oatmeal, nuts, flour. Stir in olive oil to crumb texture. Place crumb mixture on top of rhubarb mixture.

Bake at 400° for 30 minutes.

Serves 4

Ann Hooke

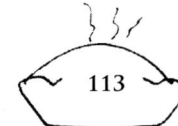

DESSERTS

Susan & Elizabeth's Gingerbread

3 cups flour, sifted
1 cup rolled oats
1 cup butter
1 1/2 cups dark molasses
1/2 cup candied lemon peel, minced
4 T grated fresh green ginger or 2 tsp ground ginger
1/4 cup cream

Heat the oven to 350º.

Cream the butter until light and fluffy, then blend in the molasses. Separately, grind oats briefly in a blender or food processor. In bowl mix in butter, flour, oats, lemon peel, and ginger. Lastly, stir in the cream.

Bake in a greased and floured 9" x 14" inch pan at 350º (I use a lasagna pan with oil and flour spray) for about 30-35 minutes.

Cut in squares to serve.

Bob Harris

"Tis an ill cook that cannot lick his own fingers."

Shakespeare, from Romeo and Juliet 1592

Cream Puffs a la Brittney

1/2 cup butter
1 cup flour
1 cup boiling water
4 eggs
1 tsp salt
3 T powdered sugar

Filling:
1 pint whipped cream

Heat oven to 400º.

Melt butter in heavy saucepan. Add flour and salt. Stir with wooden spoon until smooth. Add boiling water, all at one time. Stir until well blended, set aside to cool.

Now add eggs, one at a time, mix well after each addition of eggs.

Form into small balls and place on a greased baking sheet. Bake at 400º oven for 20-25 min.

Let the cream puffs cool, then cut off the top and fill with whipped cream. Put back lid and sprinkle with powdered sugar and serve

Brittney Kunst

Susie Wakelin's Lemon Chiffon

14 oz can sweetened condensed milk
6 oz frozen lemonade, thawed
8 oz Cool Whip
Yellow food coloring
9" graham cracker pie crust

Mix together condensed milk, lemonade and Cool Whip. Add 6 drops yellow food coloring.

Put in graham cracker crust. Chill. Can also be frozen.

Serves 6 – 8

Marjory Chesney

"An eye for an eye will only make the whole world blind."

Mahatma Gandhi

Tiramisu Sans Oeuf

24 ladyfingers
2 shots (2 oz) prepared espresso
1/2 cup prepared coffee
1 cup whipping cream
1 lb mascarpone cheese
1/2 cup sugar
3 T rum or brandy
Cocoa powder
1 oz shavings of unsweetened dark chocolate

Mix and chill espresso and coffee. Put one layer of ladyfingers in an 8" x 8" inch pan. Spread on half of the espresso and coffee. Whip heavy cream into peaks and blend in the cheese. Add sugar and rum and blend.

Spread half of the cream and cheese mixture over ladyfingers. Sift cocoa powder liberally over cream and cheese mixture. Repeat: lay on a second layer of lady fingers. Spread remaining half of the cream and cheese mixture over lady fingers. Sift cocoa powder liberally over cream and cheese mixture. Top with shavings of unsweetened dark chocolate.

Keep in refrigerator until time to serve.

Yields 8 servings

Del Rosenfield

The best thing about this is no eggs and no baking.

Deer Isle Grapenut Pudding

1/2 cup grapenuts
1 egg, beaten
1/3 cup sugar
1 tsp vanilla
1 cup dates, chopped
1/3 cup walnuts, chopped
Milk as needed

Preheat oven to 350°

Combine all ingredients and use enough milk to fill a 1-quart casserole to within 1" from the top. Set casserole dish in a larger pan of hot water.

Bake about one hour at 350° or until it starts to leave the edges of the dish, stirring once when it starts to thicken. Note: instead of using sugar, you may add 1 tsp nutmeg, and 1/2 tsp cinnamon with extra dates.

Serve with whipped cream or maple syrup over the top.

Serves 4 - 6

Eliza Spencer

This is from my nephew, Charlie Childes.

Cranberry Pies

1 pkg cranberries (4 cups)
1 cup sugar
1 cup chopped nuts
4 eggs
2 cups sugar
2 cups flour
1 1/2 cups melted butter
1 tsp vanilla
1 tsp almond extract

Pre-heat oven to 325°

Mix cranberries, 1 cup sugar and nuts, and spread in three greased 8" or 9" pie plates. Beat eggs, add 2 cups sugar slowly and beat until smooth. Add the flour and melted butter and flavorings. Pour over the cranberries.

Bake at 325° for 40 minutes.

Yields 3 pies

Jackie Dunbar

"When preparing several batches of pie dough, roll out between sheets of plastic wrap. Stack the dishes in a pizza box and keep box in freezer. Pull out the required crusts as needed."

Gluten-Free Bûche de Noël

6 eggs, separated into whites and yolks
1 cup sugar
4 oz German chocolate, melted carefully
1 pint whipping cream
1 tsp vanilla, plus 1 tsp for the whipped cream
Cocoa powder for dusting
Pinch of salt

Heat oven to 350° with rack in the middle of oven.

Beat yolks to pale yellow, add 1/2 cup sugar very slowly, still beating,

Melt chocolate gently over simmering water in a double boiler, and let cool. Butter a jelly roll pan (make sure it has edges, not a flat cookie sheet). Line with wax paper, butter it again on top of wax paper.

Using a separate bowl, beat whites to peaks and slowly add remaining half of sugar. Blend the melted, cooled chocolate into the yolks; add vanilla. Fold gently mixture into beaten egg white mixture. Add the pinch of salt. Spread the whole thing into the prepared pan and bake 15-20 minutes. Don't overbake!

Remove from the oven and cool on rack, dusting the top of the cake with the cocoa powder and then covering the cake with a damp dish towel. Wait 10-15 minutes while cake cools.

Prepare a spot on your counter with wax paper, and then flip the pan over (after you have removed the dish towel of course). Gently peel off the wax paper that the cake baked on.

Gluten-Free Bûche de Noël
(continued)

You are now ready for the fun part. Turn the cake so that the long way faces your waist as you face the counter. Now whip the cream quite stiff (but not butter) and add some sugar and some more vanilla to taste, or rum, or any flavoring you want. Spread this carefully on the cake (making sure the cake is sufficiently cooled) and then beginning at the short end, roll her right up. I like to have a platter prepared, so that the last "flip" ends on the platter and the "seam side" is down.

At this point you might want to pour yourself a glass of wine.

Frosting or Icing the log: I don't do this step. I serve it with chocolate sauce. I make cute little meringue mushrooms. My mom spreads chocolate frosting on so it looks sort of like bark on a log.

Serves 10 - 12

Eliza Childs

It looks pretty darn cute if you put a sprig of holly on the platter or greenery of some kind, at Christmas time, or you can also sprinkle some confectioners sugar on the log to resemble snow.

This cake freezes well, but I would put the confectioners sugar on after it is thawed and at room temperature.

Eagle Island Easy Fruit Tarte

Crust:
1/2 cup softened butter
1/4 cup brown sugar
1 cup flour
1 T water

Filling:
6 oz cream cheese, softened
1/2 cup sour cream
1/2 cup powdered sugar

Preheat oven to 400°.

Blend crust ingredients and form into a ball
Press with fingers the ball into 9" pie plate
Bake for 10 minutes at 400° and allow to cool

Cream together filling and chill about 4 hours.

Spread filling on crust, then decorate with sliced fruit. You may wish to melt some currant jelly and poor over the top to make a shiny presentation.

Avery Dickinson

This is not only delicious but a beautiful looking dessert.

Arlene's Pie Crust & Ottsie's Pies

2 cups all-purpose flour
1/2 cup vegetable shortening
1/2 cup butter
Blend with old fashioned pastry blender
   or with two knives.
1/2 cup milk which has 1 T of vinegar
   as part of the measurement

Add soured milk and mix with large pastry fork. Roll out on floured board. Place bottom crust on greased and floured pan. Fill. Then roll top crust, lay on pie, bring lower crust edge over top crust and trim and crimp edges. Brush top with milk and bake about 425° for about 40 minutes. Finish off at 325° for about 20 minutes more. Cool to desired serving temperature.

Apple Pie Filling:
Use native apples, peeled and sliced to fill the pie pan full and a bit more.
1 cup sugar
3/4 tsp cinnamon
1/4 tsp nutmeg
Dots of butter to dot pie, before adding top crust

Blueberry Pie Filling:
4 - 5 cups blueberries
2 tsp lemon juice

Makes 2 crusts for 8" or 9" pies.

Pies serve 6 - 8

Mayotta Kendrick & Arlene Sylvester Kydd

These contributors liked their crusts "short" and their fillings "juicy."

Bible Study Carrot Cake

2 cups flour
1/2 T baking soda
2 tsp baking powder
1 T cinnamon
1 tsp salt
2 cups grated carrots
1/2 cup crushed drained pineapple
1 1/2 cup vegetable oil
1 cup brown sugar
1 cup white sugar
4 eggs, slightly beaten
1/2 cup walnut, pecan or filbert pieces

Heat oven to 350º.

Cream sugar, oil and eggs with hand mixer. Combine flour, baking soda, baking powder, salt and cinnamon. Beat dry ingredients into moist mixture. When mixed together, stir in the carrots, crushed pineapple and nuts. Pour batter into greased and floured 9" x 13" cake pan.

Bake at 350º for 30 - 45 minutes, until tests done in center. Cool before frosting.

Frosting:
1/2 cup butter, softened
8 oz cream cheese, softened
1 tsp vanilla extract
1 lb confectioners sugar

Beat all frosting ingredients together until smooth. Frost cool cake and serve.

Elaine Presson

This was served at our Bible Study class.

Blueberry Dessert With Pineapple

8 oz can crushed pineapple
15 oz pkg frozen blueberries or 2 cups fresh
1 pkg yellow cake mix
1 - 2 sticks butter, cut in small cubes

Use greased and floured 9" x 13" pan. Layer pineapple, then blueberries. Sprinkle cake mix on top. Place cubes of butter over that.

Bake at 350º for 30 - 35 minutes.

Serves 10 - 12

Kitsy Bryant

"Yesterday is history, tomorrow is a mystery, today is a gift of God, which is why we call it a present."

Bill Keane

Billy's Coconut Cake & Frosting

For the cake:
3 cups flour
3 tsp baking powder
1/2 tsp salt
1 cup butter
2 cups sugar
4 eggs
1 1/4 cup whole milk
1 tsp vanilla

Preheat oven to 350º.

Sift together flour, baking powder and salt and set aside. Cream together butter and sugar until light and fluffy. Add eggs to butter-sugar mixture. Gradually add flour mixture to butter-sugar-eggs, alternating with milk and flavoring, but ending with dry. Beat about 5 minutes until well mixed. Pour batter into size of pans that you have chosen, greased and floured. Bake at 350º from 25-35 minutes (more or less, time will depend on size of pan used) until toothpick inserted in middle comes out clean. Makes one 9" x 13", two 9", three 8" or two 8" x 8" cakes. Single layer or double.

Coconut Frosting:
1 1/2 cup butter
3/4 cup cream cheese
1 tsp vanilla extract
1 tsp almond extract
5+/- cups sifted confectioners sugar
2 -3 cups flaked coconut, as desired

Cream butter and cream cheese together at medium speed until well blended, add vanilla and almond extract. Gradually add powdered sugar, a cup at a time, beating only until well blended. May need more powdered sugar to have good consistency. Spread on cooled cake and dust with flaked coconut.

Serves 8 - 12

Jane Nesbitt

Chocolate Macadamia Nut Torte

Crust:
2 cups crushed chocolate wafer cookies
6 T unsalted butter, melted
7 oz macadamia nuts, coarsely chopped
1 cup brown sugar
1 1/2 cups unsalted butter

Filling:
1/4 cup brown sugar
11 oz cream cheese, softened
3/4 cup confectioners' sugar

Topping:
1 cup heavy cream
1 tsp vanilla extract
8 oz semi-sweet chocolate, coarsely chopped

Preheat oven to 350º.

Combine cookie crumbs and melted butter. Press firmly into bottom of an ungreased 9" springform pan. Place the macadamia nuts in a single layer over cookie layer. Combine the cup of brown sugar with 1 1/2 cup butter and heat over medium flame until surface boils. Immediately pour over nut layer. Bake 15 to 20 minutes until surface is light brown. Remove from oven and cool on a wire rack.

Combine filling ingredients in a mixing bowl and beat until smooth. Spread over crust and refrigerate until firm. Scald the cream. Add the chocolate and vanilla and stir for 1 minute to make glaze. Remove from heat and stir until chocolate is melted and fully integrates. Refrigerate until cool enough to pour over cake without running.

Carefully run a knife around the sides of the pan and remove them. Place cake on wax paper on a plate. Spread glaze over the top and sides of cake. Refrigerate until ready to serve.

Serves 10 - 12 thin slices

Margaret Framptom

Dump-It-All-In Cake

1 1/2 quarts fruits: berries, peaches, apricots, rhubarb, etc.--fresh or defrosted, but no strawberries
1 box white cake mix
1/4 lb butter, melted
1/2 cup nuts, chopped

Preheat oven to 375º.

Dump fruit in bottom of 9" x 13" pan. Sprinkle dry cake mix over fruit. Dump melted butter over cake with spoon, making sure sides get some. Sprinkle chopped nuts over top of buttered cake mix. Just dump it all in.

Bake until slightly brown, about 30 - 35 minutes.

Serves 12 - 15

Maxine A. Peak

I sprinkled juice, from defrosted berries, on top and it looked like a cobbler. This is great with ice cream or cold whipped topping. Enjoy!

Shaker Floating Island

1 T cornstarch
4 cups whole milk, divided
5 eggs, separated
1/2 cup sugar
1/2 tsp rose water or vanilla extract
1/2 tsp salt
3 T sugar
Large pan of boiling water

Combine 1 T cornstarch with 2 T milk. Scald remaining milk in large saucepan. Beat egg yolks in a small bowl. Add cornstarch mixture and 1/2 cup sugar to egg yolks.

Stir in half the heated milk into the bowl. Then stir all cornstarch, sugar, egg yolk and first half of milk, into the remaining milk in saucepan. Cook over low heat stirring constantly for 3 minutes. Add 1/2 tsp rose water (or vanilla). Pour into serving dish and cool.

Beat egg whites very stiff. Add salt and sugar. Drop whites mixture by spoonfuls into boiling water for 2 minutes. Remove with slotted spoon and float on the custard. Chill.

Serves 6

Abby Fuller

This recipe is from The Best of Shaker Cooking, co-authored by my mother-in-law Persis Fuller. She lived in our house in Sunset in the 1950's and early 60's with Andy's father, Wolcott "Woody" Fuller.

This recipe is from Hancock Shaker Village, a Shaker museum in Hancock, Mass. Persis directed the kitchen and Good Room where baked goods, jams, jellies, etc. were sold.

Burnt Cove Blueberry Cake

3/4 cup sugar
1/2 cup shortening
2 egg yolks (save the whites)
1 1/2 cup flour
1 tsp baking powder
1/4 tsp salt
1/3 cup milk
1 tsp vanilla
1 1/2 cup blueberries
2 egg whites
1/4 cup sugar
1 tsp good cinnamon
1/3 cup white or brown sugar

Preheat oven to 350º

Cream 3/4 cup sugar with 1/2 cup shortening. Add egg yolks and beat well. Mix together flour, baking powder and salt. Mix milk and vanilla together in another bowl. Add wet and dry alternately to creamed mixture. Stir after each addition. Fold in flour dusted blueberries. Beat the egg whites with 1/4 cup sugar. Gently fold sweetened well beaten egg whites into the mixture last.

Scrape batter in 8" x 8" greased and floured baking pan. Sprinkle with cinnamon and sugar mixture before baking.

Bake at 350º for 50 - 60 minutes. Cut 3 x 3 to get 9 pieces.

This is a small cake suitable for brunch or dessert.

Norma Morey

Coffee Angel Food Cake

1 cup cake flour
1/2 cup white sugar
1/2 tsp salt
1 1/4 cups egg whites (10 - 12)
1 1/4 tsp cream of tartar
1 cup white sugar (more)
1 T powdered instant coffee or instant espresso
1/2 tsp vanilla extract
Butter icing with 2 T powdered coffee
Toasted almonds, slivered or chopped

Add 1/2 cup of sugar to flour. Sift together 4 times. Set aside.

Add salt to egg whites and beat with flat wire whisk or rotary egg beater until foamy. Sprinkle cream of tartar over the room-temperature eggs (60º - 70º) and continue beating to soft-peak stage. Add the remaining cup of sugar by sprinkling 1/4 cup at a time over egg whites and blending carefully into mixture, about 20 strokes each time. Fold in coffee and vanilla flavorings. Spread flour-sugar mixture over egg whites, about a fourth at a time and fold in lightly, about 20 strokes each time.

Pour into ungreased, round 10" tube pan. Bake at 350º for 35 to 45 minutes.

Remove from oven and invert pan on cooling rack. Ice cooled cake with butter icing, adding 2 T powdered coffee to recipe. Whip until light and fluffy. Spread on cake and sprinkle generously with toasted nuts.

Serves 10 - 12

Norma V. Sheard

This is a little fussy but worth it.

Pecan Caramel Custard

8 tsp finely chopped pecans
1 cup sugar
2 T water
2 cups milk
1 tsp vanilla
1 cup sugar
4 beaten eggs
Raspberries, mint leaves, whipped topping for garnish

Heat oven to 325°.

Put 1 tsp of finely chopped pecans into each of 8 custard ramekins.

Heat 1 cup sugar with 2 T water on medium heat, stirring often. As soon as sugar turns light brown, remove from heat. Pour into dishes; set aside.

Scald milk with vanilla and 1 cup sugar. Stir hot milk into 4 beaten eggs. Pour egg mixture evenly into each dish.

Transfer to a hot water bath. Bake at 325° for 30 minutes. Cool in refrigerator overnight. Turn out onto 8 plates.

Garnish with raspberries & mint leaves, and with a dollop of whipped topping.

Serves 8

Susan Perez

Summer Berry Sorbet

1 pint or more lemon sorbet
2 cups of fresh summer berries, without stems
8 mint leaves, to chop
4 splashes of a fruit liqueur
4 mint sprigs for garnish

Mix berries, liqueur and mint very gently. Let sit a few minutes while scooping lemon sorbet with a melon baller or ice cream scoop. Place balls in pretty individual serving dishes. Spoon fruit mixture on top of sorbet balls. Place in freezer until 10 minutes before serving. Take out and add cleaned mint sprigs, waiting in a glass of water crisping, and serve.

I have used lime and raspberry sorbet but I prefer the lemon. I also like to use a # 40 portion scoop. Scoop size 40 holds a portion of 1 3/5 T and makes uniform balls. You may omit liqueur....as you like! My Maine sister likes a splash of fresh citrus juice, especially lime, on each, in place of the liqueur.

Serves 4

Meghan Wakefield

Mrs. Washburn's Pineapple Pudding

1 stick of butter, room temperature
3/4 cup sugar
4 eggs
1 cup crushed pineapple, well drained
5 slices of bread cubed

Heat oven to 350º.

Cream butter and sugar, add eggs, and beat well. Fold in pineapple and add bread cubes.

Bake in buttered bread pan or casserole dish for 40 - 60 minutes.

Serves 4 - 8

Susan Perez

This bread pudding complements my Easter ham very nicely. Serve it with ice cream or whipped cream and you have a fantastic dessert!

Old-Fashioned Carrot Cake

1 1/2 cups sugar (brown and/or white)
1 cup vegetable oil
1 tsp vanilla extract
3 eggs
1 1/2 cup all-purpose flour
1 1/4 tsp baking soda
3/4 tsp salt
3 tsp ground cinnamon
2 1/4 cups shredded carrots
14 oz can crushed pineapple
1 cup golden raisins (optional)
1 cup walnut pieces (optional)

Preheat oven to 325º.

Cream sugar, oil and vanilla with mixer. Add eggs, one at a time, blending after each one, until smooth. Mix dry ingredients, flour, baking soda, salt and cinnamon, in another bowl. Fold dry ingredients into egg mixture. Add carrots, drained pineapple and desired optional ingredients. Stir together.

Grease and flour a Bundt pan or a 9" x 13" pan. Scrape batter into pan.

Bake about 40 - 50 minutes, until a center-inserted toothpick comes out clean.

Cool cake in pan on rack. If desired, frost with favorite cream cheese frosting, dust top with confectioners sugar, or eat plain.

Serves 12 - 15

Barbara Kingman Chesney

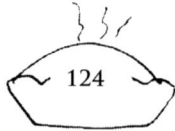

Warm Rice Pudding ("Julegrød")

1 cup rice
Dash of salt
6 cups milk
1/2 cup raisins
2 eggs
1/2 cup sugar
1 tsp vanilla extract
1/2 cup heavy cream
1/4 tsp ground nutmeg (optional)
1/4 tsp ground cinnamon (optional)

Cook the rice and salt in the milk for about 1 hour. After it just comes to a boil, turn it down quickly to a simmer. Be careful to stir often over low heat or it will burn on the bottom. Add a little more milk if needed. Add raisins last 15 minutes.

Remove from heat. Beat eggs with sugar and desired spices and then add vanilla and heavy cream. Add to cooked rice mixture. Check for seasoning and flavor.

Put pudding in a nice heat tolerant glass dish and sprinkle with sugar and cinnamon on top, if desired. Serve warm.

Serves 4 - 6

Anette Jaquette

This is a favorite at Christmas dinner in Denmark.

My grandmother put the boiling pot of rice in her featherbed where it sat all afternoon. When she took it out of the bed it was totally cooked.

Simple Elegance for Chocoholics

1 baked and cooled brownie, preferably dense
4 - 6 small rectangles of plain chocolate candy bar
Dip of vanilla or chocolate ice cream
Chocolate sauce for drizzling on top

Place the brownie on a microwaveable serving plate and top with rectangles of the chocolate bar.

Microwave until the chocolate just starts to melt, about 30 - 40 seconds depending on power of the microwave (you can do two at a time, it just takes a bit longer). The chocolate should be soft, but not dripping over the sides. Test it with a light finger touch to be sure it is warm enough.

Top with ice cream and drizzle with chocolate sauce. Serve immediately.

Serves 1

Marsha Johns

DESSERTS

Peachy Pie

1 1/2 cups unbleached flour
1/2 tsp salt
1 stick butter
2 T sour cream
Food spray or a little additional butter for the pie pan
3 perfect, ripe peaches, cut into nice slices
3 large egg yolks, beaten
1 cup sugar
2 T unbleached flour
1/2 cup sour cream (be generous here)

Preheat oven to 425°.

Process in a food processor the flour through the sour cream, until it forms a ball. Then pat this softish ball into a prepared 9" pie pan, fluting the edges prettily if you have the patience. Bake 10 minutes. Remove from oven and allow to cool while you are making the rest of the pie.

Turn oven down to 350°.

Arrange the peaches perhaps in concentric circles within the pie crust.

Now you are ready to prepare the rest of the filling. Combine the last four ingredients, mixing well, and pour over the peaches. Cover loosely with foil.

Bake at 350 for about 35 minutes or until set.

If you want to "gild the lily" you may want to melt some currant jelly (about half a cup) with 2 T Grand Marnier in a small saucepan until jelly is melted and can be poured. When you gently pour this over the top of the pie after it is baked and cooled, it gives a nice sheen to this amazing dessert.

Makes one pie

Mary Salter

Suffield Fruit Berry Cobbler

1 pint each of raspberries, blueberries, and cut-up strawberries
1 cup sugar
1 squeeze of a lemon
2 cup unbleached flour
1/4 cup sugar
Pinch of salt
1 T baking powder
1/3 cup Crisco or other vegetable shortening
3 T cold butter
1 large beaten egg
1/3 cup milk (do not use skim)

Preheat oven to 425°.

Toss all raspberries, blueberries and strawberries together and plop in a 9" x 14" buttered glass baking dish.

Crunch flour, sugar, salt, baking powder, Crisco and butter together with a pastry cutter or two forks, until the mixture looks like coarse crumbs.

Combine egg and milk with the crumb mixture, and then drop in artistically arranged clumps on top of the berries. If you want this dessert to serve nine, make nine clumps.

Bake about 25 minutes or until the clumps of dough are a pleasing golden color. This is really good when served with vanilla ice cream, or perhaps some plain Greek yogurt.

Eliza Childs

This portrait by Stanislav Remski is of Mrs. Walter ("Maggie") Gray, a past president of the "Marthas." It hangs in the balcony of the Sunset Church. Maggie was the mother of long-time parishioner, Dennis Gray.

DESSERTS

Mary Howe, Pastor Dana Douglass, and Eric Sheard

Jeannie Gresham and Sally Gillett

Chapter 8

Genesis 1:29

And God said, "Behold, I have given you every plant yielding seed that is on the face of all the earth, and every tree with seed in its fruit. You shall have them for food.

Oceanville Beef Stew

2 lbs stew beef
2 medium onions, chopped
1 lb can tomatoes chopped
3 T quick cooking tapioca
10 1/2 oz beef broth, undiluted
1 garlic clove, minced
1 T parsley flakes
1 bay leaf
6 medium carrots, cut in strips
6 medium potatoes, peeled and quartered
1/2 cup sliced celery
2 1/2 tsp salt
1/4 tsp pepper

Cut beef into 1" cubes. In oil brown on all sides along with onions and garlic with oil in a large skillet. Add rest of ingredients and bring to a boil. Put in a 3 quart covered casserole.

Bake at 350º for 1 1/2 hours.

Serves 8

Judy Rittmeyer

"To keep oil from splattering, sprinkle a little salt or flour in the pan before frying."

Breast of Chicken in Cream Sauce

2 T unsalted butter
2 large whole chicken breasts, boned, skinned and cut in strips, 1" x 3" inches
1 T minced fresh oregano, or 1 tsp dried oregano
3/4 cup dry white vermouth
2 garlic cloves, minced
1 cup heavy cream
1 tsp freshly grated nutmeg
4 - 5 oz imported Parmesan cheese, freshly grated
2 T chopped fresh Italian parsley plus for garnish
1 T fresh lemon juice
Salt and pepper to taste

In a 10 - 12-inch skillet, heat the butter over moderately high heat. When the butter begins to foam, add the chicken and oregano. Do not crowd the chicken or it will not brown. Saute for 3-5 minutes until chicken is lightly browned but not cooked all the way through. Be careful to regulate the heat so that the butter does not burn. Remove the chicken to a warm platter and tent it with foil.

Add the vermouth to the skillet. Over high heat, deglaze the pan, stirring well, scraping up the drippings. Add the garlic and boil over moderately high heat until the liquid is reduced by half. Add the cream, reduce the heat and simmer until cream has thickened slightly to a sauce-like consistency. Add the nutmeg, cheese, parsley, and lemon juice. Stir until the cheese is melted.

Return the chicken to the sauce to finish cooking and heat through. Season to taste with salt and pepper. Sprinkle with parsley. Serve with rice.

Serves 4

Paul Loggins

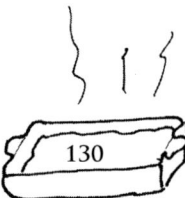

Meghan's Pesto Chicken

3 whole chicken breasts
1/2 cup mayonnaise
2 T pesto
1 1/2 cup grated Parmesan cheese
1 cup bread crumbs

Preheat oven to 400°.

Place mayonnaise and pesto in a zip lock plastic bag in the morning and mix them together. Split chicken breasts into halves and pounded a little to tenderize. Place chicken breasts into bag and squish coating over the chicken. Leave all in bag and place in refrigerator until about half an hour before serving.

Remove chicken from bag and roll in the cheese mixed with the crumbs. Place on baking sheet covered with foil for easier clean up. Place sheet in heated oven and bake for about 20 minutes or until done for the thickness of the breasts.

Note: I sometimes use fancy mustard and/or fresh herbs, such as tarragon in place of the pesto. Because this has pesto and is so easy peasy, this is my favorite chicken dish.

Serves 6

Meghan Wakefield

All Day Beef Stew

1 can sliced carrots, drained
1 can small onions, drained
1 can potatoes, drained
1 can beef broth
4 T tapioca
1 T brown sugar
1/2 cup prepared bread crumbs
1 bay leaf
1/2 cup white wine
15 oz can diced tomatoes, including juice
2 lbs stew beef cut in pieces
1 /2 T salt
1 tsp pepper

Combine all ingredients and place in crock pot on low all day.

Serves 6 - 8

Nancy Eaton

"Never overcook foods that are to be frozen. Food will finish cooking when reheated."

Charlo's Party Lasagna

1 1/2 lbs ground beef
1 1/2 T vegetable oil
1 clove garlic minced
1 T parsley chopped
2 tsp Italian seasoning including oregano
1 tsp basil, crushed
20 oz can stewed tomatoes
6 oz can tomato paste
10 oz package lasagna noodles
2 cups ricotta cheese
1 cup cottage cheese
2 eggs beaten
1/2 tsp black pepper
2 tsp salt
2 T parsley
1/2 cup plus 2 T Parmesan cheese, grated
4 oz shredded mixed Italian cheeses with Asiago
1 lb mozzarella cheese, shredded

Brown ground beef in oil. Drain. Add garlic, parsley flakes, basil, and salt. Mix with tomatoes and tomato paste. Simmer, uncovered, till thick, about one hour; stir occasionally. Cook lasagna noodles as directed on package; drain and rinse in cold water.

Preheat oven to 375°.

Mix cottage cheese with beaten eggs, pepper, and parsley flakes. Place half of noodles in 9" x 13" baking pan. Spoon on half ricotta, cottage cheese, egg and parsley mixture. Place a layer of mozzarella and other cheeses with a bit of the Parmesan; then spoon on layer of meat mixture. Repeat layers, ending with layer of mozzarella on top. Sprinkle casserole with remaining Parmesan cheese and a bit of Italian seasoning. Bake for about 40 minutes until bubbly.

Serves: 12

Charlo Davis

Really Good Pumpkin Stew a la Shirley

15 oz can pinto beans, juice reserved
14 tomatoes, peeled, seeded, chopped, juice reserved
3 ears cooked corn (cut off kernels)
1 tsp cumin seeds
1 tsp oregano
1" piece cinnamon stick or ground cinnamon
3 whole cloves
4 T vegetable oil
1 large onion, chopped medium
2 cloves garlic, finely chopped
1 T paprika
3 cups any broth or water
4 cups pumpkin, peeled and cut into 1" cubes
8 serrano peppers, seeded and finely chopped

In a small heavy skillet, toast the cumin seeds until their fragrance emerges. Add oregano and quickly transfer spices to a large bowl so they don't burn. Combine them with the cinnamon and the cloves and grind to powder in an electric spice mill.

Heat oil in skillet and sauté onion briskly over high heat for 1 minute. Lower heat to medium. Add garlic, spices, paprika and one tsp salt. Stir well to combine and then add 1/2 cup reserved bean broth or stock and cook, stirring occasionally until onion is soft. Next, add tomatoes and heat 5 minutes. Add pumpkin along with 1 cup of broth or stock. After 20-30 minutes, or when the pumpkin is about half cooked, add corn, beans, and fresh chilies. Then add reserved tomato juice, adding more broth or stock as necessary. Cook until pumpkin is tender. Check seasoning, and add more salt if necessary. Serve garnished with chopped cilantro or parsley. Even though there is corn in the stew, corn bread or tortillas make a good accompaniment.

Serves 6

Shirley Banner

Chicken Marbella

4 1/2 lbs chicken cut up
1 head of garlic
1/3 cup dried oregano
Coarse salt and ground pepper to taste
1/2 cup "wine" vinegar
1/2 cup olive oil
1 cup pitted prunes
1/2 cup green olives
1/2 cup capers with a bit of juice
6 bay leaves
1 cup white wine
1/4 cup Italian parsley
1 cup brown sugar

Mix all together, cover and let marinate in refrigerator overnight. Place in 9" x 14" baking pan.

Sprinkle brown sugar over the top and bake 1 hour at 350°, basting every 15 minutes.

Serves 10 - 12

Jean Flanders

"It's easier to slice meat thinly if it's partially frozen."

Easy Lamb Stew

3 lbs lean lamb, cut from the leg, in 1" cubes
1/3 cup flour for dredging
Salt and pepper to taste
1/3 cup olive oil
2 cups consommé, more or less
1/3 cup sherry, more to taste
2 cloves garlic, crushed
3 T lemon juice
3 T fresh parsley, chopped

Heat oven to 350°.

Dredge lamb with seasoned flour. Heat oil and sauté lamb until browned on all sides. Stir in remaining ingredients, except lemon juice and parsley; heat.

Transfer mixture to 2-quart casserole, cover and bake until lamb is tender, about 1 1/2 hours.

Stir in lemon juice and garnish with parsley.

Note: I use rice flour to make it gluten-free.

Serves 6 - 8

This is especially nice to serve with Israeli couscous.

Jean Gresham

MAIN DISHES

Family Meat Loaf-Crockpot

2 eggs, beaten
3/4 cup milk
3/4 cup dry bread crumbs
1 oz envelope dry onion soup mix
2 lbs lean ground beef

Line crock pot with a wide strip of aluminum foil, coming up the sides of the pot. This helps remove the meat loaf when done.

In a large bowl combine eggs, milk, bread crumbs and soup mix. Mix well and then add the ground beef. Mix thoroughly.

Shape into a rectangle or oval that won't touch the sides of the crock pot. Place in crock pot, cover and cook for 6 hours on low or 3 hours on high.

Serves 6

Robin Spencer-Laurie

"If you like garlic, go ahead and toss a few cloves in the water when boiling potatoes."

Prosciutto, Asparagus, and Mushrooms

1 lb nice fresh asparagus, tough ends removed
1/2 - 1/4 C mushrooms such as cremini or shiitake, sliced
2 oz. prosciutto, sliced thin, and cut into strips of about 1/4" wide
2 T good quality olive oil
Kosher salt to taste
Freshly groumd black pepper to taste
Ground nutmeg to taste, about 1/2 teaspoon
Generous pinch of dried tarragon

Preheat oven to 200 degrees.

With parchment paper, line your baking sheet (the kind with edges) with parchment paper, allowing twice as much as the pan is long.

Plop the asparagus in the center, putting them "fore and aft" so some tips point in one direction, some in the other. Plop the prosciutto and the mushrooms on that. Next pour the **2T** olive oil over all, being sure to coat all evenly, then add all the seasonings.

The parchment paper now needs to be folded and stapled (or tied with string). Bake for 1 hour.

Unwrap carefully and serve all this on a nice bed of fluffy couscous.

Serves two as a main course or four when used as a side dish.

Edie McClure and Nancy Munn

Frikkedeller
(Danish Meatballs)

1/2 lb ground lamb
1/2 lb ground beef
1 lb ground pork
1/4 cup flour
1 tsp salt
1/2 tsp pepper
1 medium onion, grated
2 eggs, slightly beaten
1/3 cup milk
1/2 cup water
4 T margarine

Mix first 7 ingredients together thoroughly. Add eggs, milk and water.

Melt margarine in a large frying pan at medium heat.

Use a large serving spoon to scoop out a spoonful of meat mixture. Drop into frying pan. Turn over when brown.

Serve with new potatoes and Danish red cabbage.

Serves 4 - 6

Lisbeth Nielsen

My Mother's Ham Loaf

3 lbs smoked ham, ground
3 lbs lean pork, ground
2 lbs lean beef, ground
1 1/2 tsp pepper
1 (28 oz) can tomatoes, drained and cut up
2 1/2 cups saltine crumbs, finely ground
5 eggs
1/2 cup milk
2 cups brown sugar
2 tsp ground mustard
1 cup white vinegar
1 1/2 cups water

Heat oven to 325°.

Combine ground meats. With your hands mix thoroughly together with pepper, tomatoes, saltine crumbs, eggs and milk. Place in 3 greased bread pans and indent the top of each loaf with a "valley" down the length of each ham loaf.

Make a basting sauce with brown sugar, ground mustard, white vinegar and water.

Bake at 325° for 1 1/2 hours, basting throughout with the sauce. Serve with potatoes au gratin.

Serves 16 - 20

If you wish to freeze the loaves, bake loaves for only 45 minutes, cool and freeze. Partially defrost the loaves and bake for 1 hour or less.

Kenna Haines

I remember my mother, Claudia Haines, served her ham loaf at dinner on our back porch in Missoula, Montana to the dashing Walter Van Tilburg Clark, author of "The Track of the Cat" and "The Ox-Bow Incident."

Pasta e Fagioli

1 T olive oil
1 onion, chopped
2 cloves garlic, finely chopped
1 stalk celery, chopped
1 carrot, peeled and chopped
1 T dried basil
2 tsp dried oregano
Dash of red pepper flakes
1 1/2 cups chopped tomatoes, with juices
3 cups low sodium chicken stock or vegetable stock
1 can northern white beans, drained and rinsed
1 cup tiny pasta shells (ditalini)
2 T fresh chopped parsley
Grated Parmesan and black pepper for garnish

In a large heavy pot, heat olive oil over medium high heat. Stir in onion and cook for 2 minutes. Stir in garlic, celery, and carrots and cook for 3 minutes. Add dried basil, oregano, and red pepper flakes and toss to coat. Stir in tomatoes and stock and bring to a boil.

Reduce heat and simmer for 30 minutes. If necessary add an additional cup of stock or water and stir in the beans and tiny pasta. Simmer for 6 - 8 minutes or until pasta is tender. Stir in parsley and serve hot with grated Parmesan and ground black pepper.

Serves 6

Judy Rittmeyer

Stuffed Pasta Shells

12 uncooked jumbo pasta shells
14 oz jar spaghetti sauce
1 cup light ricotta cheese
4 oz nonfat cream cheese, softened
1 cup shredded Italian 6-cheese
1/2 cup frozen cut leaf spinach, thawed and drained
Garlic salt to taste

Heat oven to 350º.

Cook pasta shells to desired doneness as directed on package. Drain. Spread 1 cup spaghetti sauce on bottom of 2 quart ungreased 8" x 12" baking dish.

In medium bowl combine ricotta cheese, cream cheese, 3/4 cup shredded cheese, spinach and garlic salt. Mix thoroughly.

Fill each cooked shell with two generous tablespoons of cheese mixture. Place shells in dish. Spoon remaining sauce over shells. Sprinkle with remaining shredded cheese. Cover with sprayed foil. Bake 25 - 35 minutes in 350º oven until thoroughly heated.

Serves 4

Eliza Spencer

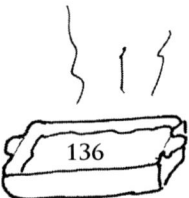

Giuliano's Moroccan Chicken

3 cloves garlic, minced
2 T olive oil
1 1/2 tsp ground cumin
1 tsp kosher salt
1/2 tsp turmeric
1/2 tsp paprika
1/2 tsp cinnamon
Ground black pepper, to taste
6 chicken legs or thighs
1 cup kalamata olives, pitted
12 dried pitted dates
1 preserved lemon*

Combine spices (garlic, oil, cumin, salt, turmeric, paprika, cinnamon & pepper) in a large bowl. Add chicken and coat well. Let stand, loosely covered, for one hour.

Place a deep, heavy skillet over medium heat. Coat lightly with oil. Add chicken; cover and cook for 20 minutes.

Discard lemon pulp; cut peel crosswise into 1/4" strips. Turn chicken over, add chopped olives and split dates along with lemon peel. Cover and cook for 20 more minutes, adding water if too dry.

Serve over basmati rice or couscous.

Serves 4 - 6

*You make preserved lemons by quartering lemons lengthwise, placing in an airtight noncorrosive container, freeze for 8 hours, add 2 T salt, store airtight at room temperature for 6 days. Refrigerate.

Calvin Massey

Wonderful Meatloaf with Sauce

2 slices bread
1 cup milk
1 1/2 lbs ground beef
2 eggs, beaten
1/4 cup minced onion
1 tsp salt
1/2 tsp sage
1/8 tsp pepper
1 small can mushroom soup (you could use celery)
3 T brown sugar
1/4 cup catsup
1/4 tsp nutmeg
1 tsp dry mustard

Soak bread in milk; mix to break bread into small pieces. Add other ingredients and mix thoroughly.

Shape into loaf and spread with mixture of brown sugar, catsup, nutmeg and mustard.

Bake 1 hour at 350º.

Serves 6

Carol Bischoff

I also use other meatloaf recipes but this is the sauce I always use. You can vary the ingredients (for example: regular mustard for dry) and just mix them in the measuring cup.

I usually bake the meatloaf about 40 minutes, then carefully pour off any grease, and then pour this topping over and bake 20 minutes more so you get less grease and more sauce flavor.

MAIN DISHES

Pete Chesney's Rare Rib Roast

1 Rib Roast (with at least 5 ribs)

Preheat oven to 500º.

Place roast, bone-side down, in roasting pan. Do not cover.

Roast 6 minutes per pound.

Turn off oven and do not open oven door for one hour (after the 6 minutes per pound has passed).

Servings depend on the size of the roast and number of hungry diners.

Serves 6 - 8

Anne Dickinson Chesney

A rib roast is an investment and this unique method of preparation helps insure that it turns out beautifully for your special meal.

Chicken with Spiced Cherries

2 tsp salt
1/2 tsp celery salt
1/2 cup brown sugar
1 cup red wine
14 oz can sweet or tart cherries, drained
1 piece whole ginger, peeled
1/2 cup tarragon vinegar
2 cloves of garlic
2 whole cloves
1 tsp basil
1 tsp oregano
4 boneless, skinless, chicken breasts
1/2 lemon
1 T paprika
Pepper, to taste
1 cup flour
Oil and butter combination

Combine the first eleven ingredients and bring to a slow boil. Reduce heat and simmer 20 minutes.

While simmering, prepare chicken. Cut chicken breasts in half. Rub chicken breast pieces with lemon. Combine pepper, paprika and flour in a bag or bowl and dredge chicken. Brown in oil and butter. Place in 7 1/2" x 11" or 12" casserole dish.

Cover with the marinade and allow to marinate in refrigerator for 4 hours. Longer is fine, and overnight is ok.

Cover and bake at 325º for 1 hour and serve over rice or with rice on the side.

Serves 4

Sue Banks

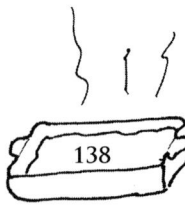

MAIN DISHES

Drunken Meat Balls

3 lb ground beef
1 large onion, finely chopped
2 - 3 garlic cloves, finely cut
1/4 cup parsley, finely cut
1/4 cup water
14 oz bottle of catsup
12 oz beer

Mix ground beef, onion, garlic and parsley until well blended. Form into small firm balls.

Brown slightly in 3 tablespoons of oil in deep pot. Add catsup, beer and water. Simmer 1 hour.

Serves 8 - 10

Pat Wiegand

"When frying meat, sprinkle paprika over it to turn it golden brown."

Winona Chang's Honey Lemon Chicken

1 chicken, cut in pieces
Flour
Olive oil
Fresh lemon juice
Honey

Heat oven to 325°.

Dredge chicken in flour. Brown in small amount of olive oil. Mix together fresh lemon juice and honey, to taste. Pour chicken drippings into honey/lemon mixture.

Place browned chicken in shallow baking pan, and pour mixture over all.

Bake at 325° until done, about an hour, depending on size of chicken parts.

Serves 4 - 6

Alice Hildebrand

Winona Chang was a good friend of my mother's and of Ruth Harris, back in NJ.

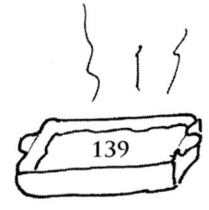

MAIN DISHES

Swedish Meatballs

1/4 cup minced onion
1 lb ground round beef
1 egg, slightly beaten
1/2 tsp nutmeg
1 1/2 tsp salt
1/8 tsp pepper

Add the above to:
1 cup of very fine bread crumbs soaked in
1/3 cup of milk.

Shape into 1-inch balls.

Sauté in 2 T of butter in skillet until lightly browned on all sides. Remove meat.

Add 2 tsp of flour to fat and blend.

Add:
1 cup of hot water
1 beef bouillon cube
1/2 cup milk
1/2 cup light cream

Cook over medium heat and stir until sauce is smooth. When thickened, about 2 minutes, add meatballs. Cover and simmer 15 minutes.

Norma V. Sheard

Little Deer Isle Roast Lamb

6 lb leg of lamb
1/2 cup Dijon style prepared mustard
2 T soy sauce
1 clove garlic, mashed
1 tsp ground rosemary or thyme
1/4 tsp powdered ginger
2 T olive oil

For honey-mustard dressing, blend mustard, soy sauce, garlic and herbs together in a bowl. Beat in olive oil by droplets to make a mayonnaise like cream.

Paint lamb with dressing mix several hours before baking.

Checking with an instant thermometer, roast in 350° oven for 1-1/4 hours until 135° for medium rare.

Serves 6

Dorothy Torrey

"You can never have enough garlic. With enough garlic you can eat the New York Times."

Morley Safer

MAIN DISHES

Pentecostal Penne

1/2 lb extra sharp cheddar
1/2 lb mild cheddar
1 lb penne
4 T butter
28 oz can chopped tomatoes with juice
1 T sugar
1 pinch salt
1 pinch pepper

Heat oven to 375°.

Cut cheese into one-inch cubes. Cook penne al dente and drain. Return to pot and stir in butter; then add the cubed cheese. Add the tomatoes, sugar, salt and pepper.

Put all in lightly buttered 2 quart ovenproof dish and bake at 375° until browned, about 40 - 45 minutes.

Serves 6

Brittney Kunst

"How do they taste? They taste like more."

H.L. Mencken

Causeway White Chili

2 chicken breasts or 12 oz can of chicken
1 T olive oil
1/2 onion
1 1/2 cloves garlic
4 oz can green chilies, chopped
1/2 tsp cumin
1/4 tsp oregano
1 dash cayenne pepper
1 can chicken broth
2 15 oz great northern beans (white)
1/2 cup Jack cheese

Cook chicken in water for 10-12 minutes (if not using can of chicken). Cut chicken in chunks. Sauté onions, garlic and chilies in oil. Add spices and broth. Bring to a boil; add beans and cheese.

Serve hot with hot cornbread or hot tortillas.

Serves 2 - 4

Anette Jaquette

My Bible study group had a chili contest and this recipe was the winner.

Bacon, Macaroni & Cheese Casserole

3/4 pkg macaroni
1 small onion, chopped
10 3/4 oz can tomato soup
1/2 lb Cheddar cheese, grated
8 strips of bacon

Preheat oven to 300°.

Cook macaroni until tender, about 8 minutes; drain and set aside. Cook bacon, drain on paper towel; set aside 1 T bacon fat. Fry onion in bacon fat.

Mix soup with a can of water and heat. Put 1/2 of the macaroni in a large casserole, layer with 1/2 the cheese and 1/2 the bacon. Repeat layers. Add onion to soup mix. Let it set 2 minutes. Pour over casserole.

Bake for about 1 hour at 300°.

Serves 6 - 8

Miriam Freeman

Beef Taiwan

1 lb ground beef
1 cup rice
1 tsp salt
2 1/2 cups boiling water
2 cups celery, cut fine
1 large onion, cut fine
1 tsp brown sugar
8 oz can sliced mushrooms, not drained
1/3 cup soy sauce

Cook ground beef in microwave. Pour uncooked rice, salt and boiling water into a 2-quart casserole. Sauté celery and onion in a small amount of butter. Add celery and onion to casserole. Add brown sugar, mushrooms and soy sauce.

Cover and bake at 350° for 1 1/4 hours or until rice is tender and liquid is absorbed. Uncover casserole for last 15 minutes.

Serves 8

David Chesney

This was one of my mother's (Peggy Chesney) favorite recipes.

"A few drops of lemon juice added to simmering rice will keep the grains separate."

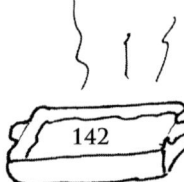

Chicken Cacciatore

3 1/2 lbs chicken, cut up
1 onion, chopped
1 tsp dried basil or oregano
1/2 tsp lemon pepper
1/4 tsp salt
2 garlic cloves, minced
1/2 cup rose wine
1 T sugar
1/2 green bell pepper, sliced
12 oz can tomato sauce
1 cup sliced fresh mushrooms
Cooked pasta

Combine all ingredients except mushrooms and pasta in slow cooker. Cover and cook on low for 5 - 6 hours.

Turn control to HIGH and add mushrooms. Cover and cook about 10 minutes.

Serve over prepared pasta.

Serves 8

Debbie Gillett Hermansen

Chicken & Apples

8 pieces of chicken breast, boned and skinned
4 slices bacon
3 apples, peeled and chopped
1 small onion, sliced
Thyme and parsley
1 cup white wine

Heat oven to 325°.

In heavy deep casserole dish (e.g., Dutch oven) fry bacon and remove. Fry onion lightly and remove. Brown chicken breasts lightly and remove. Peel and chop apples.

Place 1/2 chicken, apples, bacon, and parsley and thyme into casserole; then repeat layers. Add 1 cup white wine over all.

Bake uncovered at 325° for 1 1/2 hours.

Serves 8

Sally Gillett

"The way to a man's heart is through his stomach."

Chicken and Lentil Stew

3 tsp extra-virgin olive oil, divided
8 oz boneless, skinless chicken breast, diced
1 carrot, peeled and finely diced
4 cloves garlic, minced
2 tsp whole coriander seed, crushed
1/8 tsp salt
1/4 tsp freshly ground pepper
14 oz can reduced-sodium chicken broth
1/2 cup green or brown lentils, sorted and rinsed
6 oz bag baby spinach
1 T lemon juice
1 T chopped fresh dill

Heat 1 tsp oil in a large saucepan over medium high heat. Add chicken and cook, stirring once or twice, until no longer pink in the middle, about 2 minutes. Transfer chicken to a plate with a slotted spoon.

Add the remaining 2 tsp oil to the pan and heat over med-low heat. Add carrot, garlic, coriander, salt and pepper and cook, stirring constantly, until fragrant, 30 to 60 seconds. Stir in broth and lentils, increase heat to medium high and bring to simmer. Reduce heat to maintain a simmer and cook, stirring constantly, until the lentils are tender, 20 to 30 minutes (brown lentils take a little longer).

Add the cooked chicken, spinach and lemon juice and return to a simmer. Cook until heated through, 1 to 2 minutes. Stir in dill.

Makes 2 servings. Serve with slices of whole grain baguette and a green salad.

This recipe is from "Move It To Lose It - Healthy Island Recipes"

Eliza Spencer

Chicken Divan with Rice

3 chicken breasts, cooked and boned
16 oz broccoli, cooked and cut
3 T butter
3 T flour
3/4 cup milk
10 3/4 oz cream of celery soup, not diluted
2 cups cooked rice
3/4 cup mayonnaise
1 T curry powder
1 cup Cheddar cheese, grated

Preheat oven to 400º.

Heat butter in heavy sauce pan; when bubbly whisk in flour briefly. Add the milk and whisk until smooth and a little thicker to make the cream sauce.

Add soup, mayonnaise and curry. Mix well.

Layer rice on bottom, then broccoli and end with chicken on top in a 7" x 12" casserole. Pour the cream sauce over all. Cover casserole with grated Cheddar.

Bake at 400º for 30 minutes.

Serves 6.

Patty Elliott

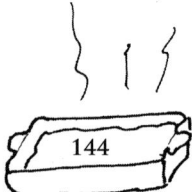

Chicken Joy

2 1/2 lbs boneless chicken breast, cut into small pieces
2 10 3/4 oz cans cream of mushroom soup
1 pint sour cream
1 cup milk
1 pkg seasoned cubed poultry dressing

Preheat oven to 350°.

Place the raw chicken in the bottom of a greased 9" x 13" baking dish. Combine wet ingredients and pour them over the chicken. Scatter the cubed dressing over the top. Bake uncovered, 45 minutes in a 350° oven or until chicken is done.

You could add mushrooms, onions, chopped red pepper or pimento for extra flavor and interest.

Serves 8

Joy Kyper

This is a tasty, easy recipe to prepare ahead of time.

"To dress up buttered, cooked vegetables, sprinkle them with toasted sesame seeds, toasted chopped nuts, canned french fried onions or slightly crushed seasoned croutons."

Country Style Spare Ribs

Sauce:
2 T salad oil
1/2 cup finely chopped onion
8 oz can tomato sauce
1 cup catsup
2 T brown sugar
1 tsp dry mustard or prepared mustard
1/3 cup vinegar or lemon juice
1/2 cup water
1 tsp salt
1/4 tsp pepper
1 T Worcestershire sauce
Bone-in or boneless pork ribs, approximately 3 - 4 lbs

Heat oven to 300°.

Place ribs in single layer in uncovered 9" x 13" pan and bake in oven for 1 1/2 to 2 hours or until brown. Drain off fat. Pour sauce over ribs, add a little water and bake 30 - 60 minutes longer. Baste occasionally.

For sauce:
Sauté onions until golden, about five minutes. Stir in remaining ingredients and simmer 20 minutes, uncovered, stirring occasionally.

All amounts can be varied. For example, less vinegar or lemon juice, as long as you get some sweet and some sour ingredients.

Serves 6 - 8

Leona Miller

This recipe quickly became a family favorite. I often double or triple the sauce recipe and freeze some for later use. It's also good served with chicken.

MAIN DISHES

Deer Isle Dal

1 1/2 cups whole black lentils, soaked overnight
1 large onion, finely chopped
1/3 cup cooking oil
2 tsp curry
2 tsp cinnamon
3 T tomato paste
1 - 2 medium-sized tomatoes, finely chopped
3 - 4 cups chicken broth, as needed
1/3 cup milk or rice milk
2 - 3 cloves of garlic, slivered
3 T butter
Salt, to taste
Cilantro leaves, snipped
1 cup heavy cream (optional)

Sauté onion till lightly brown in oil. Stir in curry, cinnamon and tomato paste. Fry about twelve seconds. Add the tomatoes and cook for a few minutes to combine. Then add the lentils and cover with the broth. Stir in the milk and let it come to a boil, and turn down to medium-low heat. Meanwhile quickly sauté the garlic in the butter in another pan. Add the cooked buttered garlic to Dal and stir into the lentils. Continue to cook for about 30 minutes until lentils are soft enough.

Stir in heavy cream at end, if using. Can omit dairy and use more broth or rice milk. Taste to see if salt is needed; adjust. Garnish with cilantro leaves.

Serve warm with cooked rice or couscous and a soft, fluffy flat bread.

Serves 6 - 8

Karen E. Crowley

Garbure

2 cups cabbage, shredded
1 clove garlic, crushed
1 envelope dry onion soup mix
2 lb can pork and beans
2 cups water
1/4 tsp marjoram
Hot dogs or little Vienna sausages from a can, cut up

Simmer all together for 1/2 hour. Serve with French bread or rolls

Serves 6

Katrina Hart

This is from France, and is a great easy dish for a tailgate picnic or such...it is really good!

"To quickly bake potatoes, place them in boiling water for 10-15 minutes. Then pierce their skins with a fork and bake in preheated oven."

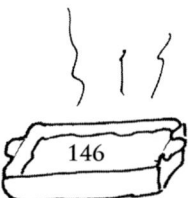

Beef and Black Bean Chili

1 lb ground round
30 oz can black beans, undrained
1 cup medium or hot chunky-style salsa
16 oz can tomato sauce
1 T chili seasoning mix
Sour cream
Shredded Cheddar cheese

Cook meat in a large saucepan over medium-high heat until meat is browned, stirring until it crumbles. Drain, if necessary.

While meat cooks, drain and mash 1 can of beans. Add mashed beans, undrained beans, salsa, tomato sauce, and seasoning mix to saucepan; stir well. Cook over medium heat 10 minutes or until thoroughly heated.

Garnish with sour cream and shredded Cheddar cheese.

Yields 7 cups

Judy Rittmeyer

"To avoid toughened beans or corn, add salt midway through the cooking time."

Spanakopita (Greek Spinach Pie)

20 oz baby spinach
2 bunches scallions
1 1/2 lbs feta cheese
6 eggs
1 lb salted butter
1 lb frozen phyllo dough sheets, thawed in refrigerator overnight

Preheat oven 350°.

Chop spinach. Finely cut scallions and put in large mixing bowl. Crumble feta cheese and beat eggs. Add one stick melted butter and mix all well. Melt other three sticks of butter, set aside and keep warm. Unroll one sleeve of phyllo dough sheets and keep covered so they don't dry out. Butter the bottom of a 13" x 9" pan. Gently place one sheet of phyllo in the pan and lightly butter. Continue this until you have eight buttered phyllo sheets layered. Sprinkle about a cup of spinach and cheese mixture onto the phyllo sheet. Filling will not cover the whole sheet. Place one phyllo sheet over the top, lightly butter it and place a second phyllo sheet down. Press lightly to smooth out the lumps in the filling and then butter the top sheet. Sprinkle another cup of filling and continue the process of layering and buttering the sheets until you have used up all the filling. The dish will be about 10 layers. Cover the last layer with eight very well buttered sheets. Bake at 350° for one hour until it is golden brown and has risen out of the pan. Remove from the oven and let stand 20 minutes to settle back down before cutting.

Serves 10 - 12.

Demetrius Pezarius

Demetrius gave us permission to use this award-winning recipe that appeared in the Ellsworth American on March 10, 2011.

MAIN DISHES

Jan Taylor welcoming new members 2011

Barbara and Jim Chesney, Rick and Jennifer Russell, and Mary Ellen Fahs;

Jan Taylor, Nick and Lisa Witte, Karen and Ned Hill

CHAPTER 9

VEGETABLES & SIDE DISHES

Genesis 1:29

Every moving thing that lives shall be food for you. And as I gave you the green plants, I give you everything

VEGETABLES & SIDE DISHES

Krispy Kale

1 bunch kale, ribs removed; tear leaves into 1"
Olive oil, enough to coat leaves
Salt, to taste

Preheat the oven to 350º.

Wash and dry the pieces of kale using a salad spinner. Put the pieces in a large bowl and toss with olive oil to coat. Arrange kale on a baking sheet in a single layer (not too much overlap, or they won't crisp). Sprinkle with sea salt.

Bake at 350º for 15 minutes, until crisp. Serve warm.

Serves 3

Del Rosenfield

This is a recipe from our granddaughter, Kat Anderson. It is simply amazingly light and crispy.

Broccoli with Orange Sauce

20 oz pkg broccoli spears, or fresh broccoli
1/4 cup butter, cubed
1 tsp cornstarch
1/2 cup orange juice
1 T grated orange peel

Cook broccoli according to package directions. Meanwhile, in a small saucepan, melt butter. Whisk in cornstarch until smooth. Gradually stir in orange juice; add orange peel. Bring to a boil; cook and stir for 2 minutes or until thickened. Drain broccoli; drizzle with sauce.

Serves 4

Carol Bischoff

I usually make more of the orange sauce and peel since we like the orange accent. I have also made this with some lightly sautéed onions, which adds some interest.

"A lump of sugar added to water when cooking greens helps vegetables retain their fresh color."

VEGETABLES & SIDE DISHES

Delicious Deer Isle

Creamed Corn a la Donnis

2 pkgs frozen corn or 1 large bag
1 cup whipping cream
1 cup milk
6 tsp sugar
1 tsp salt
2 T flour
2 T butter, melted

Mix together and add to corn.

Boil for 5 minutes and serve.

Serves 8

Donnis Lantz

I serve this dish at Thanksgiving; it is rich and so good.

"Peace begins with a smile."

Mother Teresa

Corn Soufflé Casserole

1 can whole kernel corn
1 can cream-style corn
2 eggs, beaten
1 cup sour cream (evaporated milk or whipping cream)
1/4 cup sugar
1/2 tsp pepper
1 tsp salt
1/2 cup corn oil
1 pkg corn muffin mix, small size

Preheat oven to 350°.

Mix everything except sour cream together in bowl. Then carefully fold in the sour cream. Pour into 8" x 8" x 2" square oven-proof glass pan. Bake for 45 minutes or until golden brown.

Remove and let settle 5 minutes.

Serves 6 - 8

Jackie Dunbar & Virginia Gresham

Great for church suppers, as it is easy. We learned this recipe while Virginia was sailing on the schooner, Brilliant, from Mystic Seaport, CT to Portland, ME. Be prepared to share this recipe with all. Nice to keep sour cream in the fridge and corn muffin mix on the shelves so that you can make it at the drop of a hat.

Sister Mary's Zesty Carrots
(Hancock Shaker Village)

6 carrots
Salt
2 T grated onion
2 T horseradish
1/2 cup mayonnaise
1/2 cup bread crumbs, buttered
1/4 tsp salt
1/2 tsp pepper
1/4 cup water

Heat oven to 375º.

Clean and cut carrots into thin strips. Cook until tender in salted water; place in 6" x 10" baking dish.

Mix together grated onion, horseradish, mayonnaise, salt, pepper and water. Pour over carrots. Sprinkle with 1/2 cup buttered crumbs.

Bake about 15 minutes in a moderately hot, 375º oven.

Serves 4 - 6

Abby Fuller

This is from the Best of Shaker Cooking. Co-authored by my mother-in-law, Persis Fuller.

Vegetable Casserole

1 cup slivered almonds
1/4 lb bacon, cut in 1-inch pieces
3 T vegetable oil
1 lb sliced zucchini
1 lb sliced eggplant
1 large onion, sliced
1 T flour
2 cups fresh tomatoes, or 1 lb can tomatoes, with liquid
1 tsp minced garlic
1 tsp basil
1 pkg sliced swiss cheese
1 1/2 tsp salt
1 tsp pepper

Heat oven to 400º.

Saute' almonds with bacon until brown. Drain. Add vegetables and heat over medium heat for 15 minutes. Mix in flour; add tomatoes. Stir in spices.

In a 9" x 13" baking dish, layer vegetable mix, almonds, bacon, cheese, ending with bacon and almonds on top.

Bake uncovered for 15 - 20 minutes, or until bubbly.

Serves 12

Dottie Bonnet

Danish Red Cabbage (Rodkaal)

1 medium red cabbage, shredded
1 rounded T butter
1/2 cup white vinegar
1/4 cup sugar
1/4 cup currant jelly (optional)
1 apple cut into slices
1 tsp salt

Melt butter in a large pot and add cabbage and vinegar, salt, sugar and apple. Cook gently until tender.

Season to taste with additional vinegar and sugar or some fruit juice.

Serves 8

Anette Jaquette

Red cabbage is always served with pork in Denmark.

Sunshine Summer Squash

2 lbs yellow squash (approximately 4)
1 large onion
Milk to cover squash
1 egg
Salt and pepper to taste
Cracker crumbs or breadcrumbs
1/2 stick of butter

Heat oven to 350º.

Cut onion and squash; boil in milk until tender. Mash. Add salt, pepper and egg. Sprinkle breadcrumbs on top of casserole and dot with butter.

Bake in 350º oven for 30 minutes.

Serves 4 - 6

Brittney Kunst

"Fresh lemon will remove onion scent from hands."

VEGETABLES & SIDE DISHES

Zucchini "Cakes"

2 cups shredded zucchini
1 cup bread crumbs
1 egg beaten
1 tsp mustard
1 1/2 tsp Old Bay seasoning
1 T mayonnaise
Juice of 1/2 lemon
1/4 cup chopped parsley

Mix all ingredients and form into 6 - 8 patties. Refrigerate to firm up. You could add some crabmeat too.

Heat a bit of oil in pan, flip when browned on one side.

Serve with curry mayonnaise.

Serves 3 - 4

Anne Douglass

A B C Vegetable Casserole

10 oz pkg frozen cut Asparagus
10 oz pkg frozen chopped Broccoli
10 oz pkg frozen Cauliflower
10 3/4 oz can cream of mushroom soup
3 oz can French fried onion rings.
3/4 cup cheddar cheese, shredded

Preheat oven 350°.

Thaw veggies in microwave or 2 - 3 hours on the counter. Drain well and mix in a large bowl. Spray a 2 quart casserole dish with vegetable spray. Place veggies on bottom of dish. Cover with soup, then cheddar cheese. Push soup and cheese down into the veggies. Cover and cook for 45 minutes. Top with onion rings and cook, uncovered, 15 minutes.

Serves 8

Eleanor Eaton

"To save money, pour all vegetable cooking water into a freezer container. When full, add tomato juice, any leftover vegetables, season, and create a "free" soup."

Basil Pesto, Squashed Tomatoes

6 medium to large tomatoes
1 medium yellow squash
1 medium zucchini
2 T olive oil for sautéeing
2 T basil pesto
3 large green onions, snipped thinly
1 1/2 cups good cheddar cheese, grated
1 cup Parmesan cheese, grated for topping
Salt and pepper to taste

Set oven to broil.

Cut bottom end off each tomato, remove the insides, set upside down on rack or paper towel to drain.

Cut squashes into small pieces and lightly sauté in olive oil with the pesto, just until tender.

Remove sauté pan from burner, add green onions, cheese, salt and pepper, and spoon into tomatoes. Sprinkle Parmesan on top. Place stuffed tomatoes in oven pan, place in hot oven and broil until cheeses melt.

Alternate good cheeses to use are: mozzarella, feta, Gorgonzola, blue or Asiago; grated or crumbled.

Serves 6

A nice summer dish that I like to serve on the farm when the ingredients are plentiful.

Meghan Wakefield

"Vinegar can remove spots caused by tomatoes. Soak the spot with vinegar and wash as usual."

Cheesy Potatoes

1 T butter to rub oven dish
8 potatoes, peeled and sliced
1 cup sour cream
Few drops Worcestershire sauce
Few drops balsamic vinegar
2 - 3 T cream
1 cup grated cheddar cheese
Salt and pepper to taste
Few sprinkles of garlic powder
1 medium onion, chopped small
Parmesan cheese, to sprinkle on top

Preheat oven to 350°.

Rub 9" x 13" oven dish with butter.

Boil potatoes approximately 5 minutes until almost done and drain. Layer half of the potatoes in the oven dish, sprinkle with 1/3rd of the cheese. Sprinkle with salt, pepper, and garlic powder. Add a few drops of Worcestershire sauce, balsamic vinegar, the chopped onion and 2 - 3 T cream to the sour cream. Spread half of the enhanced sour cream over the potatoes and grated cheese. Layer the rest of the potatoes on top. Cover with second third of cheddar cheese, add the rest of the enhanced sour cream. Sprinkle top with Parmesan cheese. Bake for 40 minutes covered.

Remove cover, add last 1/3rd of the cheddar cheese, sprinkle with a little more Parmesan cheese and bake another 30 minutes.

Remove from oven and let rest 10 minutes.

Serves 9 - 12

Marilyn Schroer

VEGETABLES & SIDE DISHES

Gram's Baked Beans

2 cups beans
2 T molasses
2 T ketchup
Piece of salt pork
Onion (small)

Prepare 2 cups dry beans. Pick over dry beans and wash. Place in cold water and soak overnight. Drain before putting in cooking pot.

Add molasses, ketchup, pork and onion to drained beans. Bake covered in 325º oven most of the day Be sure to keep beans covered with water, by adding as needed, so that they won't boil dry.

Serves 6 - 8

Susan Perez

Gram was Ruth Perez who preferred to use Jacob's Cattle dried beans for her baked beans.

Grazia's Asparagus Pesto

1 lb fresh asparagus, stems trimmed, chopped into 1/2" sections, cooked until tender-crisp
1 small jar of pine nuts, toasted briefly in frying pan
1/3 cup of olive oil
1/2 cup grated Parmesan cheese

Put all this in a blender and buzz it all up until it is quite smooth.

This makes a delicious sauce for pasta.

Yields 2 - 3 cups

Francesca Liberatore

A real Italian dish.

"Failure is the condiment that gives success its flavor."

Truman Capote

Nancy Torrey's Cheese Squash

4 medium summer squash
1/2 cup milk
6 T real mayonnaise
2/3 or more cup grated (extra) sharp cheddar cheese
Salt and pepper to taste

Preheat oven to 350º.

Slice squash, remove seeds, steam cook in a small amount of water, drain. Place the squash in a shallow greased casserole.

In a sauce pan, slowly stir milk into the mayo, stir in half of the grated cheese. Season with salt and pepper. Cook over low heat, stirring often until thickened. Pour cheese sauce over the squash in the casserole and sprinkle with the remaining cheese.

Bake until brown and bubbly.

Serves 6

Susan Perez

Tina's Baked Beans

16 oz white pea beans, navy beans or yellow-eye beans
1/2 lb salt pork if fat; 1/4 lb if lean, score with sharp knife, just to pork rind.
1 onion
3 T molasses
1/2 tsp powdered mustard
1/2 tsp pepper
2 tsp salt

Preheat oven to low, about 200º.

Soak beans in cold water overnight. Then parboil on the stove top until skin cracks when blown on, about 1/2 hour, or more.

Put onion in pot, then part of beans, then cross-scored pork, then the rest of beans and then molasses mixed with seasoning. Cover with boiling water. Then put cover on pot and bake slowly for 8-10 hours. Add more water after two hours and then after every other hour as needed to replace the liquid absorbed by the beans

Serves 4 - 6

Tina Howe

Clapshot

1 lb baking potatoes, peeled and cubed
3/4 lb turnips, peeled and cubed
1/4 lb carrots, peeled and cubed
1 tsp salt
2 T butter, cubed
3 T heavy cream

Place the potatoes, turnips, carrots, and salt in a Dutch oven. Fill with water to cover the vegetables and bring to a boil over high heat. Reduce the heat to medium-high and boil the vegetables until tender, 20 -25 minutes. Drain and mash the vegetables with a potato masher.

Spoon the mashed vegetables into a serving dish, top with cubes of butter and drizzle with cream.

Serves 2 - 4

Del Rosenfield

This is a very Scottish dish to be served with haggis, beef, pork, lamb or game. With the flecks of carrots, it is certainly more colorful than mashed potatoes. We are serving it for Thanksgiving this year to accompany the turkey. We will probably substitute plain fat-free yogurt for the heavy cream.

Courgettes Farcies Provençales
(Stuffed Zucchini)

2 large zucchini
2 onions sliced
2 tomatoes sliced
3/4 cup white wine
Lemon wedges
Salt, pepper, coriander seeds to taste
3 T olive oil

Heat oven to 350°.

Cover bottom of oiled baking dish with sliced onions. Cut zucchini in half horizontally; then cut each half vertically from the mid-point toward the ends of the zucchini, making 3 cuts up to 3/4 of the way down, so slices are still attached to one another.

Fill cuts with slices of tomatoes. Season with salt, pepper and coriander seeds. Place zucchini in baking dish on top of onions. Pour dry white wine half way up zucchini. Trickle olive oil over all. Cover dish with foil.

Bake for one hour at 350 °. Serve with lemon wedges.

Serves 4

Barbara Alweis

German Red Cabbage

1/2 lb bacon
1 head red cabbage, diced
2 T red wine vinegar
1 T sugar

Cook bacon until crisp and set aside. Leave bacon grease in pan. Sauté cabbage for about 5 minutes. Add vinegar and sugar. Stir for about three minutes. Add crisp bacon and mix well.

Serve as soon as it is done or reheat in microwave.

Serves 8

Virginia Schick

"Hunger finds no fault with the cooking."

Anonymous

Pumpkin Island Pumpkin

1 pumpkin - about 7 inches in diameter
4 slices of toasted bread
1/4 lb of sliced good cheddar
3/4 cup of sweet cream or milk
Salt and pepper to taste

Cut out a circle around pumpkin stem, saving the stem end. Scoop out seeds. Fill center with layers of bread and cheese. Pour in milk or cream. Cover with the saved stem end of pumpkin.

Bake at 350° on a cookie sheet for about 1 1/2 hours until knife can be inserted easily.

To serve, scoop out large spoonfuls of pumpkin meat and filling.

Serves 4

This can be served as a first course - in place of soup or salad. Or it can be the main dish for a luncheon, followed by a salad. Or it can be served as a side dish.

Barbara Alweis

VEGETABLES & SIDE DISHES

Rodbedesallad (Red Beet Salad)

16 oz jar pickled beets, drained
2 medium apples, thinly sliced and peeled
1/2 cup mayonnaise

Mix all an hour ahead and chill before serving.

Serves about 6

Katrina Hart

This is a quick Swedish side dish.

"A hungry man is an angry man."

English proverb

Stuffed Baked Potatoes

6 baking potatoes
1/2 stick of butter
1/4 cup grated onion
1/3 cup of cream
Salt and pepper to taste
1 cup shredded cheese
Snipped chives or parsley (optional)
Paprika (optional)

Bake potatoes until done, approximately 1 hour in 350° oven.

Cut potatoes lengthwise to scoop out insides. Put in bowl and mash with butter, onion, salt, pepper and cream. Fill potato skin with mashed potatoes.

Sprinkle with cheese and chives or parsley, if using. Top with paprika, if using. Bake for 20 minutes at 350° and serve.

Serves 6

Anette Jaquette

VEGETABLES & SIDE DISHES

Yam Casserole

4 large yams
1/4 cup sherry
1 T vanilla
1/2 cup brown sugar
1/3 cup flour
Walnuts, to taste

Bake, peel and mash yams. Add sherry and vanilla. Combine brown sugar, flour and chopped walnuts to create a topping.

Place in casserole dish. Bake for 30 minutes at 325º.

Serves 4

Martha Bicknell

"A woman is like a tea bag; you never know how strong it is until it's in hot water."

Eleanor Roosevelt

String Beans with an Indian Accent

1 lb fresh string beans, the skinnier the better, stem ends removed
1 tsp Kosher salt
2 tsp canola oil
1 tsp brown mustard seeds
1 medium yellow onion, peeled and chopped quite thin
2 tsp peeled fresh ginger, chopped fine

Plunge the beans in boiling salted water; cook until tender crisp, to your taste, about 3 minutes. Drain the beans.

When your large skillet is heated to hot, carefully add the oil. When this just begins to smoke, carefully add the mustard seeds, and cook until the seeds start to "pop" which should take only about 30 seconds. Stirring, add the onion and cook some more, until the onion begins to brown just a bit, about three minutes or so. Then add the ginger, cook about 1 more minute and finally add the reserved beans, and cook this all together just until everything is hot.

Serves 4

Ruth Ingham

VEGETABLES & SIDE DISHES

A lobster picnic on the beach

Flounder once plentiful in Penobscot Bay, heading for dinner table
David Jaquette, 1954

Chapter 10

John 21: 11-13

So Simon Peter went aboard and hauled the net ashore, full of large fish, a hundred and fifty-three of them; and although there were so many, the net was not torn.

SEAFOOD

Crabby Crab Cakes

1/2 cup mayonnaise
1 large egg, slightly beaten
1 T Dijon mustard
1 lb fresh lump crabmeat, drained
1 cup crumbled saltines, 25 - 30 crackers
Canola oil

Combine the mayonnaise, egg, and mustard. Mix well, then fold in the crabmeat and saltines. I place the saltines between 2 sheets of waxed paper and roll them with a rolling pin to crumble them. Let the mixture stand for about 3 minutes before shaping it into patties. This recipe makes 12 patties. Put them on a baking sheet, covered with waxed paper or plastic wrap and refrigerate for an hour.

Fry the cakes in vegetable oil, about 3 - 4 minutes on a side until they are golden brown. Drain on a paper towel and serve.

For spicy cakes, add 1/2 tsp of hot sauce to the first three ingredients. I like to serve crab cakes with a dab of mayonaise mixed with Old Bay seasoning to taste on the side. You can also make the patties small and serve them as an hors d'oeuvre.

Yields 12 patties

Katherine Hall Page

People have very strong feelings about crab cakes. They're like barbecue-beef or pork! Catsup-based or mustard-based sauce? With crab cakes, the debate starts with the crab-Maryland, Louisiana, and Maine devotees weighing in on one coast; Washington on another. Then, breading, crackers, or potato as binding? Worcestershire sauce, seafood seasoning, Tabasco or all three to complement the crustacean? Celery? Onions? The above is the recipe my family prefers after many happy trials. We like our crab cakes crabby with as few additions as possible. This recipe appeared in one of my mysteries.

Baked Stuffed Haddock

1 lb haddock
2 T lemon juice
2 T white wine
2 tsp dried rosemary or more if fresh
2 T butter
16 Ritz crackers
Parsley, fresh or dried

Heat oven to 350°.

Place haddock in shallow, greased baking dish, skin side down. Pour lemon juice, then wine, over fish. Crush rosemary and sprinkle over fish.

Melt butter. Crush crackers and add to butter and mix with a fork. Spoon cracker mixture on top of fish. Bake 20 minutes or until fish is flakey.

Garnish with parsley, fresh or dried.

Serves 3 - 4

Dick Davis

My son called for this recipe the night he was making dinner and proposing to his future wife. The dinner turned out well, she accepted his proposal, and this recipe helps us reflect on the memories food can have for relationships. The original recipe came from The Library restaurant in Portsmouth, NH.

"Lemon juice rubbed on fish before cooking will enhance the flavor and help maintain a good color."

Jackie Dunbar's Baked Haddock

Haddock (allow about 1/3 lb per person)
Butter for drizzling on top
Bread crumbs
Lemon pepper seasoning

Preheat oven to 500°.

Grease pan well. Season fish with lemon pepper seasoning. Shake bread crumbs to coat haddock. Put haddock in greased pan. Drizzle with butter.

Bake for 10 minutes.

Jackie Dunbar

" Give a man a fish, and you feed him for a day. Teach a man to fish, you feed him for a lifetime."

Chinese proverb

Crab Cheese Puff

4 slices of buttered bread
8 oz container of crabmeat
1/2 lb cheddar cheese, shredded

Blend the following and set aside:
3 eggs
2 cups milk
1/2 tsp dry mustard
1/2 tsp salt
1/3 tsp pepper

Heat oven to 325°

Layer 1/2 of the bread, crab meat and cheese in a buttered casserole dish and repeat. Pour the blended liquid mixture over the top. Bake for 40 - 50 minutes until well set.

Serves 4

Barbara Rice

"He was a brave man that first ate an oyster."

Jonathan Swift

Howard Corning's Mill Island Crab Whiffle

4 slices white sandwich bread
1 cup milk
1/4 cup butter, melted
1/2 lb crabmeat
3 eggs

Preheat over to 350º.

Tear bread into small pieces and place in 9"square greased baking dish. Add milk; soak briefly. Add melted butter and add crabmeat. Beat eggs and add. Stir to combine.

Bake 45 minutes at 350º.

Serves 2 - 4

Jean Flanders

"Fish to taste right, must swim three times - in water, butter and in wine."

Polish proverb

Steven's Sweet and Sour Shrimp

1/4 cup olive oil
1/2 cup chopped onion
3/4 cup chopped celery
3/4 cup chopped green pepper
2 T flour
1 cup tomato or vegetable juice
6 T brown sugar
1/2 tsp salt
1/4 cup lemon juice or lemon zest
1 lb rinsed Maine shrimp

Place olive oil in large skillet. Heat over medium heat. Add chopped onion, chopped celery, chopped green pepper. Sauté for 3 - 4 minutes. Stir flour into vegetables. Add the tomato or vegetable juice; stir mixture until slightly thickened. Add brown sugar, salt, and lemon juice (or zest). Stir gently until brown sugar dissolves.

Rinse shrimp and then add to skillet. Gently simmer an additional 2 to 3 minutes. Serve over rice.

Serves 2 - 3

Ann Hooke

Steven is Nita and Chandler Barbour's son.

Ray's Crab Cakes

1 lb crabmeat
3/4 cup sautéed diced onions
2 well-beaten eggs
2 tsp mustard
1/2 tsp Worcestershire sauce (optional)
1 tsp salt
Dash of pepper
1 cup Ritz cracker crumbs

Chop and sauté onions and set aside.

Combine crabmeat, onions, eggs, mustard, Worcestershire sauce, and Ritz cracker crumbs. Add salt and pepper. Form into cakes.

Fry in butter for about 5 minutes (until browned), turning once.

Yields 12

Mary Ellen Fahs

Sand Beach Ginger Mussels

4 T sesame oil
3 T minced fresh ginger
4 cloves garlic, minced
4 scallions, sliced thin
4 T soy sauce
2 cups dry white wine
1 cup low sodium chicken broth
4 lbs mussels, scrubbed, beards pulled free and discarded
2 T cornstarch mixed with 1 T water
1/2 cup chopped cilantro

In large sauce pan over medium heat, combine oil, ginger, garlic. Stir 1 minute then remove from heat. Add scallions, soy sauce, wine and broth.

Add mussels to sauce, cover and bring to a boil; reduce heat and simmer just until mussels open, stirring after 2 minutes. Transfer mussels from pan to heated serving bowl with slotted spoon. Cover and keep warm. Do not use any unopened mussels. (You already knew that.)

Stir cornstarch mixture into cooking liquid. Don't worry. It won't be lumpy. Boil, stirring constantly; mix in cilantro. Pour mixture over mussels and serve immediately.

Serves 6

Jake Garrels

It is nice to have some hot baguette with which you can sop up the elixir.

Roast Shrimp Plus

6 plum tomatoes, about 1 lb
2 medium onions, about 12 oz
2 medium zucchini, about 8 oz
Salt to taste
1/4 tsp cayenne pepper, or to taste
4 T butter or olive oil
1 1/2 lbs peeled shrimp
1/2 cup roughly chopped basil

Heat oven to 500º.

Chop the tomatoes, onions and zucchini into roughly 1/2 inch cubes, and combine them in a large broad skillet or casserole. Add salt, cayenne and half the butter or oil; place in oven. Roast 10 - 15 minutes, shaking the pan once or twice.

Remove the pan from the oven and stir well; at some point, the tomatoes will break up and become saucy (If this does not happen, roast another 5 minutes).

Add the shrimp. Roast 5 minutes, then stir and add remaining butter or oil. Roast until shrimp are pink and firm, about 5 minutes more. Taste and adjust seasoning, stir in basil and serve.

Serves 4

Zach Rosenfield

This is my favorite recipe. It is easy to prepare in advance, and can be put in the oven after guests arrive since it takes only 20 - 25 minutes to cook.

Maine Fish Chowder

4 oz fatback*, cut into 1/4 inch chunks
1 onion sliced thin
4 white potatoes, unpeeled
1 lb lean fish like cod, haddock or hake, cut into 3" x 4" inch chunks
1/2 cup crumbled common crackers or saltines
1/2 tsp salt
1/8 tsp black pepper
12 oz can evaporated milk

In a heavy pot over medium heat, cook fatback until nearly crisp. Add onions, stir, and reduce heat to low. "Chip" a potato by holding it in one hand and turning it slowly while using a sharp paring knife to cut quarter-moon-shaped quarter-inch-thick slices directly into pot, creating an even layer. Chips will have a thick end which will remain intact, and a thin end which will dissolve and thicken broth. Repeat with remaining potatoes.

Add fish in an even layer, then crumbled crackers in an even layer. Do not stir. Add cold water until it nearly covers layers. Sprinkle with salt and pepper, cover, and simmer until potato is tender, about 15 minutes. Remove lid, add evaporated milk, bring to a simmer, and stir. Serve with additional crackers, if desired.

Total cooking time is about 20 minutes.

Serves 4

* On the island salted pork is used for fatback

Sandy Oliver

Was published in New York Times, January 17, 2007, adapted by Sandy Oliver

Penobscot Chowder

5 slices bacon, fried crisp (or salt pork)
1 medium onion, chopped
2 cups boiling water
2 cups diced potatoes
1 lb cod filets, or any cheap, white fish
1 tsp salt
10 oz can chopped clams
1/2 lb shrimp, peeled (or more)
4 cups whole milk
1 cup light cream
1/8 tsp pepper
1 T chopped parsley

Fry bacon until crisp, set aside, reserving 2 T of drippings. Saute onion in bacon drippings. Add water and potatoes. Cook until potatoes are tender.

Add filets which have been cut in 1 1/2" cubes; add shrimp, salt and simmer until fish is cooked, about 5-7 minutes.

Add diced bacon, drained clams, milk, cream, pepper and parsley. Simmer a few minutes.

Serves 8

Susie Banks

Sicilian Fish Soup

1/3 cup olive oil
1 1/2 cup chopped green pepper
1 cup chopped onion
2 cloves garlic, minced
28 oz canned chopped tomatoes
1 cup water
Potatoes to desired amount
1 tsp fennel seeds
1/2 cup white wine
1/4 tsp pepper
2 lbs cubed haddock
1/2 tsp basil
1/2 tsp thyme
2 tsp salt

In heavy pot sauté in olive oil the green pepper, onion and garlic.

Add and simmer for 30 minutes the tomatoes, water, potatoes, salt, fennel seeds, wine, and pepper.

Add the fish, basil, thyme and salt and simmer 20 minutes more.

Serves 6 - 8

Alice Hildebrand

"Scaling a fish is easier if vinegar is rubbed on the scales first."

Marshall Island Scallop Chowdah

8 - 10 peeled potatoes, cut in bite-size chunks
1 medium onion, finely chopped
2 quarts water in stock pot
1 quart scallops, nubs removed
1 12-fl oz can evaporated milk
1/2 cup (1 stick) butter
saltines, salt and pepper, as desired

Start cooking potatoes and onions in water, until they just start getting tender. Cut scallops in halves or quarters depending on size. When potatoes are tender, add the scallops. When scallops "whiten out" add evaporated milk. Add the butter at the end.

Serve with saltines and pass the seasonings.

Depending on how hungry you are this might serve 5.

Capt. Robert W. Turner, Jr.

When the winds are not blowing too hard and the snow has stopped temporarily, take your boat out with the drags hooked up. Haul the scallop drags around in a few circles, winch them up, dump everything that comes up in the dumping box, separate scallops from the other bottom stuff and return drags to floor of the bay. During the next tow, start shelling out the scallops. Continue until the weather changes or it is time to go in. Then head for shore and dealer. Remember to reserve one quart before selling and take it home to make the chowdah. Note: Some folks just buy them.

Dick Bridges' Lobster Chowder

8 T unsalted butter
1 medium onion, chopped in 1/2 inch dice
3 large russet potatoes, peeled and cut into 1/2" cubes
6 cups lobster broth (or cold water)
1/2 tsp sea salt
1/4 tsp freshly ground black pepper
5 lbs steamed and shucked lobster, claws intact, tails cut in large bite-size pieces
3 cans evaporated milk (12 oz size)
1 tsp dried basil
1 cup milk or cream, if necessary

In a large kettle over low heat, melt 2 tablespoon butter. Add onion, stir, and cook until soft, about 5 minutes. Add potatoes and 6 cups broth or water, and bring to a simmer. Season with salt and pepper. Cook for about 30 minutes, until potatoes begin to soften.

Meanwhile, in a large skillet over medium-high heat, melt 2 tablespoon butter. Add a third of the lobster and sauté for about a minute or so. Set aside. Repeat with remaining lobster and butter.

Add lobster to onion and potato mixture; stir over medium heat. Add canned milk and basil, taste and adjust seasoning with additional salt and pepper. If mixture is too thick, add milk or cream. Serve.

Total cooking time is about 40 minutes.

Serves 12

Captain Dick Bridges

When Maine shrimp are in season in winter, I like to add a handful to the chowder. This recipe appeared in The New York Times of January 17, 2007. In the accompanying article, Ted Ames is quoted as saying, "Fishermen have always cooked on their boats. We just didn't admit it at home."

Christmas Eve Red & White Stew

2 - 3   1 1/4 lb lobsters
1 quart boiling water in bottom of pot
3 - 4 T butter
1 tsp vinegar
2 1/4 lbs shucked ocean scallops
12 oz can evaporated milk
1 cup milk
Salt and pepper to taste
Dash golden sherry (optional)

Try to get someone else, with a license, to catch the lobsters and scallops in December. Steam the "bugs" for about 20 - 25 minutes. Save 4 - 6 cups broth. Cool off and rinse the lobsters so you can pick lobster meat from claws, body and tails. Cut the meat in bite-size pieces. In a large skillet, sauté the lobster meat in butter with 1 tsp vinegar to tenderize the meat and release the rich red color. Set aside. To be elegant we often have scallops also. You can remove the nubs from 2 cups of ocean scallops, slice them up in silver dollars of about equal size to cook at the same time. Then place them in the lobster broth to cook until they whiten. When they whiten add the lobster meat. In five minutes add the milks and season to taste. Bring to steam but don't let stew boil after milk is in. Add a splash of sherry at end, to taste, or just sip while cooking.

Ladle into warmed bowls. Serve with hot biscuits, small round soup crackers or saltines.

Serves 5

Note: The important thing is to use fresh caught seafood but make in the morning to let stew ripen.

Ted Ames and Robin Alden

This is our favorite feed. We have had the lobster and scallop stew every Christmas Eve for dinner for about 10 years.

Coveside Crab Melt

1 T onion, minced
4 T mayonnaise, more or less
3 T ketchup
1 1/2 tsp Worcestershire sauce
l lb cooked and picked out crabmeat
4 English muffins
2 T butter
8 slices tomato
8 slices of sharp Cheddar cheese

Preheat oven 375º.

Mix onion, mayo, ketchup, Worcestershire sauce and a little bit of salt, if desired, with the crab. Split and butter the muffins. Put a tomato slice on each with 1/8th crab mixture on the tomato and a cheese slice on top of the crabmeat.

Bake at 350º for about 20 minutes.

Serves 4

Carol Carter

This is considered a "good one" in the Carter family.

Island Summer Cod

1 1/2 lbs fresh cod
1 T kosher (coarse) salt
3 ripe tomatoes or 8 sundried tomatoes, drain oil
2 medium onions
2 T olive oil
1 garlic clove (or garlic powder)
1/4 cup olive oil
1 or 2 green scallions, chopped
Dash cayenne pepper to taste
Herbs like basil or mint, chopped (optional)
Bread crumbs to sprinkle on top

Heat oven to 325°.

Brush cod on both sides with salt and let stand for at least two hours; refrigerate if longer. Slice onions and tomatoes, and sauté them slowly in olive oil; they should not brown; sauté them until onions are translucent.

Rub baking dish with half garlic or sprinkle with garlic powder. Drip half the olive oil over the bottom of the dish. Arrange half the slices of onions and tomatoes in the dish; you may want to brush off some of the salt if you put on a great deal of salt.

Lay the fish in the dish and cover with remaining slices of onions and tomatoes, the chopped scallions, some herbs, a touch of cayenne pepper, and a sprinkle of bread crumbs.

Drip the rest of the olive oil over all. Lay a piece of aluminum foil or baking paper on top; do not make it fit tightly since you will take it off 5 minutes or so before removing the dish from the oven. Bake the fish 10 minutes per inch of thickness. Voila!

Serves 4

Francine Dupuis

Lobster and Leek Pasta

4 cooked 1 1/4 lb lobsters
Olive oil for browning and sautéeing
4 large leeks, sliced in half and cleaned
3 carrots, peeled and chopped
8 celery stalks, chopped
2 cloves garlic, minced
1 bay leaf
1 cup dry white wine
1/2 cup chopped parsley
2 cups heavy cream
Salt and pepper to taste
1 lb dry wide noodle pasta like fettuccine

Pick tails and claws of lobsters, chop meat to 1/2" pieces and refrigerate.

To make stock, place remaining parts of lobsters, shells, legs, etc. in large pot with 3 T olive oil and brown lightly, about 10 minutes. Separate green and white parts of leeks. Clean and chop green parts and add to pot along with garlic, carrots and celery. Cook for another 3 - 4 minutes and add wine, bay leaf, 7 cups of water and 1/2 of the chopped parsley. Simmer for about 1 1/2 to 2 hours.

Slice remaining white part of the leeks length-wise into strips, rinse, clean, pat dry and then chop in 1/4" rings. Sauté in a pan with 2 tsp olive oil until soft and tender, about 8 -10 minutes.

Strain stock through a sieve and add liquid to sautéd leeks. Discard solids. Add cream and bring sauce to a boil, reduce heat to simmer for about 30 minutes. Stir often.

Cook pasta per instructions, in salted water. While pasta is cooking add lobster meat to the sauce along with the remaining parsley and heat. Add salt and pepper to taste. When pasta is cooked al dente, drain and toss with sauce. Serve at once.

Serves 6

Scott Miscione

Macaroni & Brie with Crab

Non-stick cooking spray
1 lb medium shell pasta
Water as per pasta package
1 tsp butter or oil
1 medium onion, thinly sliced
5 T butter
1/3 cup flour
3/4 tsp salt; 1/2 tsp pepper
3 cups milk
1 lb Brie cheeses, trimmed & chopped
  (leave 8 small wedges for topping)
3/4 lb of crabmeat
3 pieces white or other bread, torn and processed
  to coarse crumbs
Salt and pepper to season crumbs

Preheat oven to 350°.

Lightly coat 8 (14 - 16 ounce) single baking dishes with cooking spray. Set aside. Cook pasta, drain, stir in butter or oil and set aside in pot.

In a large skillet, cook onion in butter about 15 minutes or until tender and golden brown. Add flour, salt and pepper to onion in skillet; stir until thick and bubbly. Gradually add chopped cheese, cook over med-low heat until cheese melts. Stir in milk until smooth again and then pasta. Fold in crabmeat and put into baking dishes. Season bread crumbs with salt and pepper to taste. and sprinkle over cheesy crabby macaroni.

Bake uncovered, 20 - 25 minutes or until heated through and crumbs are golden brown. Add wedge of Brie to each dish last 5 minutes of baking.

Serves 8

Susan Perez

Maple Balsamic Salmon For Two

12 oz wild caught boneless Atlantic salmon filets
2 oz balsamic vinegar
2 oz Maine maple syrup
1 oz olive oil
Pepper and salt, freshly ground

Rinse and pat dry salmon filets. Set aside.

Put vinegar, syrup and oil in a small bowl. Add salt and pepper to taste.

Whisk all marinade ingredients together and pour into a good-sized heavy duty freezer bag. Place filets into bag, and "zip" it closed carefully. Marinate for 30 minutes, turning bag periodically to coat fish evenly.

Brush olive oil onto grid of grill. Remove salmon from bag and place onto preheated grill. Grill on medium to medium high heat approximately four minutes. Turn over and grill another 3 to 5 minutes depending upon how hot the grill is and how rare you like your fish.

Serves 2

Phelps Brown

Mussel Chowder With Veggies

2 cups water
1 cup bottled clam juice
4 lbs mussels, scrubbed with dark threads, beards removed
6 T butter
3 T olive oil
4 cups, about 1 1/4 lbs, white potatoes
1 tsp salt
1/2 tsp black pepper, freshly ground
2 carrots, peeled and roll-cut small
2 leeks, white and pale green parts, thinly sliced
1 yellow bell pepper, seeded and chopped
2 large shallots, chopped
1 T minced garlic
3/4 cup dry white wine
2 cups heavy cream or part evaporated milk

Add mussels and clam juice to large pot of boiling water. Cook covered on medium-low until they are all open (4 - 6 minutes). Discard any that don't open. Save the broth. Before shucking, put aside 16 of the mussels still inside their shells.

Cook potatoes in oil and butter on medium heat for 5 minutes in a large soup pot. Add carrots, leeks, bell pepper, and shallots. Cook covered, over low heat until all are tender, (10 minutes). Add garlic and cook, stirring 1 minute. Add wine, raise heat to high and cook briskly until reduced by about one-third (3 minutes). Add set-aside mussel broth without bottom sediment. Add cream and shucked mussels. Simmer, uncovered, for 5 minutes to blend flavors. Add mussels you saved in their shells. Season with additional salt and pepper to taste. Allow the chowder to blend its flavors for at least 4 hours. It is even much better to age it overnight.

When ready to serve, reheat gently and ladle into warmed bowls. Take the time to see that each bowl has at least 2 of the mussels still in their shells and serve.

Brooke Dojny

Brooke Dojny gave us permission to use this colorful recipe of hers that is used at Thurston's Lobster Pound on Mt. Dessert Island. She published it in her 2006 cookbook titled, Dishing Up Maine.

Peekytoe Crabmeat Rolls

1 lb lump crabmeat
1/2 cup white salad dressing or mayonnaise,
1 1/2 tsp lemon juice
6 top-cut, flat sided, white bread rolls
Butter to spread on rolls
Oil or butter for griddle
Paprika, to sprinkle on top (optional)

Gently mix crabmeat with dressing or mayonnaise. If using, add juice or vinegar. Butter one side of rolls with softened butter. Spread crab mixture along center of roll. Sprinkle tops with paprika, if using. Place on griddle and grill or "toast", buttered side down, for a few minutes until golden.

Meanwhile butter the top of the rolls while cooking on the griddle. When golden, carefully turn roll over and cook on other side.

Serve fresh and warm. Soft inside, toasted outside and oh so tasty.

Serves 6

Charlo Davis

These, pink when cooked, local crabs are very prized for texture and flavor. Once taught how, they are easy to pick out. When picked, they are our ultimate fast food.

I make my lobster rolls the same way, substituting bite-size cooked lobster meat for the crabmeat and adding 1/4 cup finely chopped celery.

Pressy Village Pesto Pasta

2 cups basil
2 cups spinach
3/4 cup Parmesan cheese
1/2 cup extra virgin olive oil
4 garlic cloves crushed to remove skins
2 tsp lemon juice
1/4 tsp pepper
2 lbs Maine shrimp--or what is available
2 T extra virgin olive oil
1 lb dry pasta of choice or availability
Parmesan and Romano cheese to sprinkle on top

Blend the first seven ingredients in a blender or food processor. Set the pesto aside. Cook and drain the pasta.

Sauté the shrimp in the olive oil. Individually or on a platter, layer the pasta with the shrimp and pesto. Sprinkle the Parmesan and Romano on top and serve warm.

Serves 4 - 6

Charlo Davis

I created this dish because I seem to like the spinach more and more as I get older. My pasta of choice now is often whole wheat. I like to make this dish because it is so tasty and quick. I have also enjoyed it with scallops.

Scallop Cheese Puff

2 cups of scallops
1/2 lb grated cheddar cheese
6 slices of bread, buttered and cubed
2 cups of milk
3 eggs
1/2 tsp dry mustard
Salt and pepper to taste

Preheat oven to 350º.

Scald scallops in hot water 1 minute. Butter a medium size casserole dish. Layer 1/3 the bread, half the scallops and half the cheese. Repeat in that order. End with bread on top.

Beat milk, eggs, mustard, salt and pepper. Pour over all.

Bake for 40 - 50 minutes.

Serves 6

Susan Perez

Puffs are often appetizers or a brunch dish. In a casserole dish like this it could be a side dish or a main dish depending on what accompanies it.

SEAFOOD

Spicy Scallop and Cauliflower Stew

2 T olive oil
1 large onion, chopped
1 large carrot, peeled, halved lengthwise, sliced
1 garlic clove, minced
1/4 tsp ground cumin
1/4 tsp dried crushed red pepper
28 oz can Italian plum tomatoes, undrained
8 oz bottle of clam juice
1/4 cup dry white wine
1/2 tsp dried thyme, crumbled
1/2 medium cauliflower head, cut into bite-sized florets
3/4 lb bay scallops

Heat oil in heavy medium saucepan over medium-low heat. Add onion and cook until translucent, stirring occasionally, about 8 minutes. Add carrot, garlic, cumin and dried red pepper and cook 1 minute.

Puree tomatoes with juices in a blender. Add to saucepan. Mix in clam juice, wine and thyme. Simmer 10 minutes. Can be prepared 1 day ahead. Cover and refrigerate. Rewarm before continuing.

Add cauliflower to stew and cook until tender, about 15 minutes. Add scallops and cook until just opaque, about 2-3 minutes.

Thicken with cornstarch as desired.

Serves 4

Mary Framptom-Price

Cod with Miso Glaze

1/4 cup mirin or other Japanese sweet rice wine
1/4 cup white miso paste
1/4 sugar, more or less to taste
Olive oil
4 skinless cod filets, no more than 6 ounces each

Combine the mirin, miso and sugar in a saucepan and whisk together over medium flame until you see that the sugar is dissolved. Then let this mixture cool.

While the mixture is cooling completely, preheat your broiler, first placing the oven rack about 6 inches from the heat. Now oil or spray your baking sheet, and place the filets on the prepared sheet and spread the miso mixture on top of the filets. Once the oven has reached "broil" heat, pop the pan in the oven and broil until filets look browned, golden on top and the centers of the filets are opaque. This will take about 6 minutes. If you find the tops are browned before the fish is cooked enough for your taste, you may cover with foil and cook a bit more.

Serves 4

Maysie Anderson

How to Prepare and Freeze Whole "in the shell" Lobster

Properly prepared whole or "in the shell" lobster has a good quality shelf-life of 9 to 12 months.

1. Lobsters should be chilled and live.

2. Blanch at 212 F for 60 seconds in a 2% salt brine (2.5 Tbsp of non-iodized or sea salt to 2 quarts of water.)

3. Chill after blanching in cold running water or in a tub with a mixture of 50% water to 50% ice.

4. Following a 15-20 minute chill, remove excess surface water.

5. Place in commercial freezer bags and remove as much air as possible. (New Ziploc vacuum bag systems available at supermarkets work well.)

6. Place in a second freezer bag or over-wrap with a laminated freezer wrap.

7. Freeze at -18 C (0 F)- standard for home refrigerator/freezer units.

8. Store frozen at -18 Cup" (0 F) or lower -the lower the storage temperature the better the lobster meat quality will be maintained.

9. Thawing directions: Lobsters should be thawed overnight in the refrigerator.

10. Thawed lobsters should be boiled in a 2% salt brine for 12-15 minutes.

You can also just freeze tails and claws "in the shell":
1. Follow steps 1 through 4 above

2. Remove claws and tail from blanched lobsters

3. Continue with steps 5 through 10 above

How to Prepare and Freeze Picked Tail and Claw Meat:
Lobster meat that has been picked and frozen will have an acceptable shelf life of 3-6 months if stored at temperatures of 0 F (-18 C) or lower.

1. Follow steps 1 through 4 above.

2. Remove tail and claw meat from the shell.

3. Place in commercial freezer bags and remove as much air as possible. (New Ziploc vacuum bag systems available at supermarkets work well.)

4. Continue with steps 7 through 10.

5. Thawed lobster meat can be prepared by steaming for 8-10 minutes (in a colander above steaming pot of water).

Lobsters can be frozen "green," or uncooked, but shelf-life is limited and off-flavors can develop.

Judy Rittmeyer, Kellie Coombs, Mary Hardy, Brenda Gilchrist, Eliza Spencer,
Nita Barbour, Carol Gotwals, Bob Coombs
Workers at OASIS Cafe on the Fourth of July serving breakfast and brunch

Oasis Cafe cooks view the parade while taking a break
from making 130 crab rolls.

Chapter 11

1 Corinthians 10:31

So, whether you eat or drink, or whatever you do, do all to the glory of God.

BREAKFAST & BRUNCH

Blue Lemon Poppy Coffee Cake

Cake:
2/3 cup sugar
1/2 cup butter at room temperature
2 tsp lemon zest
1 egg, beaten
1 1/2 cups flour
2 T poppy seeds
1/2 tsp baking soda
Pinch of salt
1/2 cup sour cream

Filling:
2 cups fresh or frozen blueberries, thawed and drained on paper towels
1/2 cup sugar
2 T flour
1/3 tsp nutmeg, freshly grated

Glaze:
1/2 cup powdered sugar and 1 - 2 T milk

Grease and flour bottom and sides of 9" or 10" spring-form pan. In large bowl beat 2/3 cup sugar and butter until light and fluffy. Add lemon zest and egg. Beat 2 minutes at medium speed. In medium bowl, combine flour, poppy seeds, baking soda and salt. Add to butter mixture alternately with sour cream. Spread batter over bottom and 1" up sides of prepared pan, making sure batter on sides is at least 1/4" thick. In another medium bowl, combine all filling ingredients; add on top. Bake 350° for 45 - 55 minutes or until crust is golden brown. Cool slightly.

In small bowl, combine powdered sugar and enough milk to make smooth glaze. Drizzle creatively over top of warm cake.

Serves 8

Lanny Anderson

Cardamom Coffee Cake

2 cups butter softened but not melted
2 cups light brown sugar
4 eggs
2 tsp vanilla extract
2 cups sour cream, plus 1 - 2 T yogurt
4 cups white unbleached all-purpose flour
2 tsp each baking powder and baking soda
1/2 tsp salt
1 1/2 tsp ground cardamom
1/4 cup light brown sugar
1 T ground cinnamon
1/2 cup pecans or walnuts, chopped

Preheat oven to 350°.

Cream the sugar and soft butter. Then add eggs, vanilla, sour cream and yogurt. Mix wet ingredients thoroughly.

In a second large bowl sift dry ingredients together: flour, baking powder, baking soda, salt and cardamom.

Add flour mixture and moist ingredients alternately, beginning and ending with flour. Mix just to blend both together.

In a small separate bowl, mix the 1/4 cup brown sugar, cinnamon and nuts together. Spoon the batter into a well-buttered, 9" or larger, tube pan. Place batter and nut crumb mixture in pan in layers as follows: 1/3 batter, 1/2 nut mixture; another 1/3 batter, the rest of the nut mixture and finally the last 1/3 of batter. Place the pan on a baking sheet to catch rising spillovers and bake for 1 1/2 hours or more until top browns and tests clean and dry on a broom straw or toothpick.

Serves 8 - 12

Allen Myers

This recipe was adapted by experience from The Moosewood Cookbook by Mollie Katzen. It is rich, dense, and special in our home.

Christmas Brunch Casserole

1 lb bacon
1 T butter
2 onions, chopped
2 cups fresh sliced mushrooms
4 cups frozen hash brown potatoes, thawed
1 tsp salt
1/4 tsp garlic salt
1/2 tsp ground black pepper
4 eggs
1 1/2 cups milk
1 pinch dried parsley
1 cup shredded cheddar cheese

Grease a 9" x 13" casserole dish.

Place bacon in a large, deep skillet. Cook over medium high heat until evenly brown. Drain and set aside. In a separate skillet, melt butter and fry onions and mushrooms until tender.

Preheat oven to 400º.

Place potatoes in bottom of prepared dish. Sprinkle with salt, garlic salt, and pepper. Top with bacon, then onions and mushrooms. In a large bowl, beat eggs with the milk and parsley. Pour over the casserole. Top with grated cheese. Cover and refrigerate overnight. Can be baked in the morning.

Bake at 400º in oven for one hour or until set.

If preparing and baking the same day, bake for 45 minutes.

Serves 6 - 12

Debbie Gillett Hermansen

Coffee Cake

2 cups flour
1 1/2 cups white sugar
1 cup butter or margarine (cold)
1 cup sour milk (2 tsp vinegar into the milk)
1 tsp baking soda
2 eggs, slightly beaten
1 tsp vanilla
Cinnamon to sprinkle on top

Heat oven to 350º.

Blend margarine, sugar and flour. Reserve 1 cup of the mixture. Add soda to sour milk, wait a couple of minutes. Add soured milk, eggs and vanilla to dry mix. Scrape batter, dividing into two 9" round greased and floured pans.

Crumble reserved mixture on top. Sprinkle with cinnamon on each.

Bake at 350º for 20 - 25 minutes until it tests done in the center.

Serves 12 - 14

Lucy Vander Mel

I like it because these ingredients are usually in my kitchen and I can decide to make it at the last minute. This cake tastes great on its own but will accept seasonal additions.

Ginger Raisin Scones

2 cups flour
2 tsp baking powder
1/2 tsp salt
1 heaping T sugar
1/2 cup butter, very cold
1 cup raisins
1/4 cup crystallized ginger
2 eggs
Enough milk to make a thick batter

Preheat oven to 450º.

Mix flour, baking powder, salt and sugar. Cut in butter with a fork or pastry cutter, stirring frequently. Add raisins and ginger and mix well. Add eggs and milk.

If dough is thick, roll out and cut; if thin, drop by spoonfuls on ungreased cookie sheet.

Bake 12 - 15 minutes, or until browned on top.

Allen Myers

"Eat breakfast like a king, lunch like a prince and dinner like a pauper."

Goat Cheese and Herb Frittata

6 eggs
Fresh sage or combination of savory, dill, thyme, or parsley, chopped and to taste.
Salt & pepper to taste
3 T butter or olive oil
1 shallot, peeled & chopped
4 oz goat cheese, crumbled
12 cherry tomatoes, halved
Spray of olive oil

Preheat the broiler. Beat together the eggs and fresh herbs in a bowl. Season with salt and pepper. Heat the butter or oil in a heavy, oven-proof skillet. Add the shallot and sauté until softened. Add the egg mixture, cover, and simmer for 10 -15 minutes. Remove lid. Frittata should be moist on top.

Arrange cheese and tomatoes over surface of frittata and spray lightly with oil. Place under broiler until browned.

Remove from skillet, cut into generous-sized wedges and serve hot or at room temperature.

Serves 4

Brenda Gilchrist

Green Tomato Breakfast Cake

1/3 cup butter, softened
1 cup sugar
2 eggs
1 tsp vanilla
1 cup flour
1 tsp baking powder
1/2 tsp ground cinnamon
1/8 tsp salt
2 green tomatoes, cored and thinly sliced
1/3 cup golden raisins
1/2 cup slivered almonds or other nuts
2 T brown sugar mixed with
2 tsp cinnamon to sprinkle on top

Spray coat a 9" round cake pan.

Preheat oven to 350º.

Cream butter and sugar in mixer. Beat in eggs and vanilla. Combine flour, baking powder, cinnamon and salt. Add the flour mixture, 1/2 cup at a time, to butter mixture; and beat well each time. Stir in the raisins and nut pieces. Fill the prepared pan with batter. Spread tomatoes on top of batter and sprinkle with sugar and cinnamon. Bake 50 - 60 minutes, until firm and golden.

Serves 8

Susan Perez

Try it and you'll like it too!

Lowe's Road Breakfast Apple Cake

2 cups sugar
1 1/4 cups vegetable oil
2 eggs
2 tsp of vanilla
3 cups flour
1 tsp baking soda
1 tsp baking powder
1 tsp salt
1 1/2 tsp ground cinnamon
3 cups peeled apples, chopped to bite-size pieces
1 cup walnut pieces

Preheat oven to 350º.

Pour oil over sugar. Add eggs and vanilla and beat well. Mix flour, baking soda, baking powder and salt together. Add these dry ingredients to the wet mixture. Beat together briefly. Add the chopped apples and walnut pieces. Stir slightly. Turn thick lumpy batter into an angel food or Bundt pan, oiled or sprayed with cooking spray. Bake at 350º for about 1 1/4 hours. Center inserted toothpick should come out clean. Cool on wire rack.

Serves 10 - 12

Susan Perez

I was a cook at The Finest Kind, a popular Deer Isle restaurant owned by my husband and myself. Priscilla Merritt was wife of the director of Haystack Mountain School of Crafts on Sunshine and worked there with Kaye Milan, both good cooks! Priscilla and I were good friends. This recipe was courtesy of Priscilla who got fruit from the Capens on Lowe's Road.

Southern (Risen) Buckwheat Cakes

Quart water, boiled and cooled to between 118° - 125°
1 1/2 cups all-purpose flour
1 1/2 cups buckwheat flour
1 pkg yeast
1 tsp salt
1 T molasses
6 T oil or melted butter
1 egg
1 tsp baking soda

Put flours, yeast and salt in 4 - 5 quart mixing bowl with the correct temperature water and mix together. Cover bowl tightly and let sit overnight. Next morning add molasses, oil or butter, egg, and baking soda and stir all well. Cook on a hot, well-oiled griddle.

Yields 72 small cakes.

Phil Miller

I have had good luck with storing the batter for as long as 10 days in the refrigerator. It is a matter of taste, but I generally prefer small cakes to large ones.

The Pancake

1/4 cup butter
1/2 cup flour
1/2 cup milk
2 eggs, beaten frothy

Preheat oven 425°.

Preheat your "spider", also known as a cast iron skillet, on middle shelf of oven. Mix all ingredients together except the butter. Beat very well. Melt the butter in the pan. Pull middle shelf out carefully and pour the mixture into pan on top of melted butter. Cook about 20 - 25 minutes, until golden. Cut in wedges. You may dust with confectioners sugar.

Serve immediately.

Serves 4 - 8

Katrina Hart

Watch it puff up.

Maggie Spofford's Crabmeat Quiche

1/4 cup onion, chopped fine
1/4 tsp salt
1/8 tsp cayenne pepper
1 tsp sugar
4 eggs, slightly beaten
2 cups whipping cream
1 1/2 cups shredded Swiss cheese
1/2 lb crabmeat
Unbaked 8"- 9" single pie shell

Heat oven to 425º.

Mix ingredients together.

Pour into unbaked pie shell. Sprinkle with paprika on top.

Bake at 425º for 15 minutes. Then reduce heat to 325º for approximately 40 minutes.

Serves 6

Susan Perez

Oeufs en Cocottes à la Polly

Butter for greasing the custard cups
6 T of prepared pâté, homemade or canned
6 large eggs
6 T shallots, chopped and sautéed
6 T mushrooms, chopped and sautéed
Salt and pepper, to taste
Enough heavy cream to cover

Preheat oven to 350º.

Butter 6 4-oz ovenproof custard cups. Place one T pâté in each prepared cup. Top with an egg, chopped and sautéed mushrooms, shallots, salt, pepper, and enough heavy cream to cover.

Place cups in flat pan, at least 9" x 13", with a towel on bottom. Place hot water in pan that has lemon juice to keep pan from discoloring, and add enough hot water to come halfway up outside of custard cups for gently cooked eggs.

Bake 12 - 15 minutes, until whites of egg have become slightly firm.

Serves 6

The Rev. Sarah Winn Nichols

Polly says this is even good without the pâté which she often omits.

Versatile Griddle Cakes

2 cups flours, including grain germs
5 tsp baking powder
2 tsp salt
3 T sugar
2 eggs
2 1/4 cups milk or buttermilk
1/3 cup vegetable oil
Sweet syrup, maple syrup or cinnamon-sugar

Some possible variations:
Spiced: 1/2 tsp ground cinnamon with orange or lemon juice, as part of liquid, and zest
Corn: 1 can 7 to 8 oz whole corn-use liquid as part of juice, or creamed corn
Banana: 2 mashed ripe medium sized bananas
Any Berries: 1 cup fresh or rinsed frozen berries with a 1/4 tsp ground. cinnamon
Chocolate Chips: 1/2 cup itsy chocolate bits
Apple: 1 cup finely chopped raw apple with 1 tsp ground cinnamon and 1/2 tsp nutmeg and occasionally 1/3 cup roughly chopped nuts

Add mixed dry ingredients to wet and hand mix. Check batter for thickness. Adjust by adding liquid if too thick. Heat griddle. If needed, grease griddle before each batch. Drop batter by tablespoon, for minis; 1/4 cup for 4" cakes on hot greased griddle or pan. Flip when bubbles start to stay open. Cook on other side. Serve with sweeteners of choice.

Makes about 16 4" pancakes.

Frank Davis

After many years of being breakfast or breakfast buffet cook on the island, my wife still makes many versions of my basic recipe. Our daughter, Cheryl, prefers the corn! Her son, Nick, prefers the chocolate bits. The "Grands" prefer the mini pancakes.

Caramel-soaked French toast

2 cups firmly packed brown sugar
1 cup butter
1/4 cup maple syrup
10 slices (1 3/4 inch thick) French bread
6 large eggs
3 1/2 cups of milk
1 T vanilla extract
1/4 tsp salt
3 T sugar
1 1/2 tsp ground cinnamon
1/4 cup butter melted

Combine first 3 ingredients in a saucepan. Cook over medium heat, stirring constantly for about 5 minutes. Pour syrup mixture into a lightly greased 13x9x2 inch baking dish and arrange bread slices over syrup. Combine eggs and next 3 ingredients: stir well. Next pour mixture over bread slices. Cover and chill overnight.

Combine 3 T sugar and cinnamon: stir well. Sprinkle evenly over soaked bread. Drizzle 1/4 cup melted butter over bread. Bake, uncovered at 350° for 45 to 50 minutes.

Serves 10

Grethe Nielsen

Elizabeth Harris Seater and Keith Wood
at the Sunset Village Green Memorial Garden. (2005)

BREAKFAST & BRUNCH

In the hammock are the younger generation from these families:
Hermansen, Wakelin, Gresham, Nichols, Hutchins, Childs, Chesney,
Palmer and Vaughn

Vernon and Carol Gotwals our organist and choir director 1984 to 2001

CHAPTER 12

THIS and THAT

SPREADS, RELISHES, COMPOTES, SAUCES, CONDIMENTS, ETC.

1 Corinthians 10:31

So, whether you eat or drink, or whatever you do, do all to the glory of God.

5 Minute Chocolate Mug Cake
(The most dangerous cake in the world)

4 T flour
4 T sugar
2 T cocoa
1 egg
3 T milk
3 T oil
3 T chocolate chips (optional)
Small splash of vanilla extract
1 large coffee mug (microwave safe)

Add dry ingredients to mug, and mix well. Add the egg and mix thoroughly. Pour in the milk and oil and mix well. Add the chocolate chips (if using) and vanilla extract, and mix again. Put your mug in the microwave and cook for 3 minutes at 1000 watts.

The cake will rise over the top of the mug, but don't be alarmed! Allow to cool a little, and tip out onto a plate if desired.

Serves 2

Stella Wiens

This is well named the most dangerous cake recipe in the world because, now we are all only 5 minutes away from chocolate cake at any time of the day or night!

This is fun to make with very young children. It is also possible to make in messy college dorms, bachelorette or bachelor pads.

Mitli* Chili Lime Peanuts

6 T lime juice
6 T chili powder
4 tsp kosher salt
1/2 - 1 tsp cayenne pepper
6 cups unsalted cocktail peanuts

Preheat oven to 250º.

Position racks in the upper and lower thirds of oven. Whisk lime juice, chili powder, salt and cayenne in a large bowl. Add peanuts. Toss to coat. Divide between 2 large rimmed baking sheets, spread in an even layer.

Bake, stirring every 15 minutes, until dry, about 45 minutes. Let cool completely.

Store in an airtight container.

Yields 6 cups

Calories per 2 T serving is 110 calories.

Eliza Spencer

Courtesy of Move It To Lose It recipes by Healthy Island Project.

Bordeaux Relish

2 quarts green tomatoes, chopped
1 quart cabbage, ground
3 large onions
3 red peppers
2 oz mustard seed
1 T celery seed
1 T turmeric
4 cups sugar
3 T salt
1 quart vinegar

Cook all ingredients together slowly until well heated.

Yields 16 small jars

Eliza Spencer

Original recipe from Nancy Eaton. This is great on hot dogs and hamburgers.

"Hunger is the best sauce in the world."

Cervantes

Osprey Point Nutty Granola Bars

3/4 cup honey, divided
2 T butter, plus more for baking dish
3 cups old fashioned rolled oats
1 1/2 cups slivered almonds, toasted, for more flavor
Coarse salt
1 cup raisins, chopped dried apricots, or other dried fruit
1/3 cup creamy peanut, almond or cashew butter
1/4 cup light brown sugar

Preheat oven to 325°. In a small saucepan heat 1/4 cup honey and butter over low. Cook, stirring until butter melts, about 2 minutes.

In a large bowl, combine oats, almonds and pinch of salt. Drizzle honey mixture over oat mixture and stir to combine; wipe saucepan clean. Spread mixture evenly on a large rimmed baking sheet. Bake for 20 minutes or until golden brown, stirring occasionally. Let cool completely on sheet, about 10 minutes. Return to large bowl and add raisins; stir to combine.

Lightly butter an 8" or 9" square baking dish. In saucepan, combine 1/2 cup honey, peanut or almond butter, and brown sugar over medium heat. Cook, stirring occasionally until mixture comes to a boil and sugar dissolves, about 10 minutes. Immediately drizzle over the oat mixture and stir until combined. Transfer to baking dish.

With a spatula firmly press granola into dish. Refrigerate until firm, about 1 hour and then cut into 16 - 20 bars or squares. Store in airtight container at room temperature up to 5 days.

Bill Johns

These are a great snack to carry in lieu of store-bought bars.

This & That

Ellen's Fruit Dip

Combine in saucepan:
1/2 cup pineapple juice (drained from 1 can)
1/4 cup lemon juice (usually 1 lemon)
1/2 cup white sugar
2 eggs, well beaten before adding
8 oz carton whipping cream, whipped

Cook over medium heat until thick, stirring constantly. Cool and refrigerate. Mix with whipped cream prior to serving. If you like it really lemony, add less whipped cream. Keeps in refrigerator for several days. Serve with pineapple chunks, strawberries, sliced bananas, melon balls, apple slices, or green grapes. Makes two generous bowls of dip.

Ellen Harries

I'm Carol Bischoff's walking partner and friend; I serve this at elegant book signings in Florida and it always works well.

Horseradish & Mustard Sauce

1 T chopped onion
3 T butter
2 T flour
1 cup milk or light cream
1/4 cup prepared horseradish, or 3 T prepared mustard and 1/2 tsp Worcestershire sauce

Brown 1 tablespoon chopped onion in 3 T butter. Add 2 tablespoon flour, then 1 cup of milk or light cream to make a sauce. When thick, add 1/4 cup prepared horseradish.

To make mustard sauce, substitute 3 tablespoons prepared mustard and 1/2 tsp Worcestershire sauce and serve over fresh pork, spareribs or ham.

Norma V. Sheard

"Salt is born of the purest of parents: the sun and the sea."

Pythagoras

Very Best Pie Pastry

2 cups sifted flour
1 T sugar
1/2 tsp baking powder
1/2 tsp salt
1/3 cup lard (room temperature)
1/3 cup butter, unsalted (room temperature)
1 large egg, slightly beaten (4 T)

Combine dry ingredients; sift into bowl. Cut in lard and butter until dough is the size of peas. Add egg, one tablespoon at a time, pushing damped clumps to the side. Save the last tablespoon for crumbs at the bottom.

Gather and knead lightly until consistent. Divide in half, patting each half into one inch thick round. Wrap in plastic wrap; refrigerate overnight.

I double this recipe, wrap the next day in foil, and freeze. I always have pie dough on hand.

Nancy Hodermarsky

I received this recipe from my dear friend, Penny Binswanger.

Zucchini Pepper Relish

5 lbs of zucchini
1 green pepper
8 large onions
1 T ground nutmeg
1 T dry mustard
2 1/2 cups vinegar
2 tsp celery or seasoned salt
4 cups sugar
1 tsp turmeric
1 sweet red pepper
1/3 cup salt

Wash zucchini; cut up. Peel and quarter onions. Put through a food grinder, but not too fine, I like mine a little chunky. Put in a large non-metal bowl. Combine ground zucchini and onion with salt; mix well and set aside overnight.

Next day, wash and rinse jars, keep hot. Drain vegetables thoroughly. Rinse them with cold water. Drain again. Combine all ingredients in a large kettle and heat to a boil. Reduce heat and simmer for 30 minutes, stir occasionally.

Put in hot jars, filling to 1/2 inch from top. If you run short of liquid, you can add a bit of vinegar. Put lids on. Process in boiling bath 30 minutes, or pressure cook them at 10 pounds for 10 minutes.

Makes 6 - 8 pints, depending on amount of onions used.

Margie Nevells & Holly Meade

Marinade for Chicken

1/3 cup soy sauce
1/3 cup canola oil
1 T honey (warmed)
2 cloves garlic, chopped
1 tsp ground mustard
1 lb boneless, skinless chicken breasts

Combine soy sauce, canola oil, honey, garlic and mustard in a bowl and stir until well mixed.

Add chicken parts, marinate overnight, turning chicken occasionally to coat all parts.

Grill and serve.

Serves 4

Dick Davis

We often make a double batch of this and freeze the chicken in the marinade so it's ready to grill when thawed. We sometimes add ground or fresh minced ginger as well. The marinade makes the chicken very tender and even kids find it easy to eat.

Mother's Watermelon Pickle

4 lbs or 8 cup watermelon
2 lbs or 4 cup white sugar
1 pint or 2 cup cider vinegar
1 1/2 T cinnamon
2 tsp cloves
1 T allspice

Cut off outside rind and all soft pink melon. Cut rind that's left in bite-size chunks. I cut it up smaller for eating with steak.

Boil till soft, about 10 minutes. Drain.

Add sugar and spices to melon rind in pan. Simmer 10 minutes. Put immediately in sterilized jars. Wipe top of jars clean. Use clean rubber rings or metal tops that are new. Just leave on counter, out of drafts, till cool.

If you prefer, you may tie whole spices in a bag. I don't, even though my mother did. I like to eat this with horseradish and a good steak, mac and cheese or grilled cheese sandwiches.

Jan Gordon Rosati

The recipe is from Helen Gordon of Deer Isle. People still mention how lovely and useful the church music stand is that Al and I contributed in her memory. She loved music and the church.

THIS & THAT

Cranberry Orange Piquant

12 oz cranberries
2 cups sugar
1 cup mandarin oranges, drained
1 cup apples, unpeeled, chopped coarsely
1/2 cup raisins
1/2 tsp cinnamon
1/2 tsp ginger
1/2 cup nuts, chopped coarsely
1 T vinegar

Combine all ingredients in medium saucepan. Cook until the berries begin to burst. Refrigerate or freeze.

The original recipe you may cook in the microwave, but for big batches use stovetop.

I take great liberty in altering the proportions. Getting proportions of the sweet and tart make it interesting. I usually make a double batch and freeze much of it in smaller containers.

Carol Bischoff

This is our traditional holiday dish with turkey, and now family favorite, even better than the jellied version we all like!

Claudia's Fudge

4 1/2 cups sugar
12 oz can evaporated milk
1 pint marshmallow creme
14 oz chocolate bar
1 lb semisweet chocolate chips
1 or more cups walnuts, chopped
1/4 - 1/2 cup butter, not melted

Bring the sugar and the evaporated milk to a boil and boil for exactly 2 minutes. Remove from heat and add marshmallow creme, chocolate, walnuts and butter. Mix well and pour into large greased pan. Cool before cutting.

Yields 5 lbs fudge

Kenna Haines

My mother's fudge recipe was given to me by Anne Maclay on her sheep ranch in Lolo, Montana.

Two-Tone Fudge

2 cups brown sugar, packed
1 cup sugar
1 cup evaporated milk
1/2 cup butter or margarine
7 oz jar marshmallow crème
1 tsp vanilla
6 oz pkg butterscotch flavored pieces (1 cup)
1/2 cup nuts, chopped
6 oz pkg semisweet chocolate pieces (1 cup)
1/2 cup nuts, chopped

Combine sugars, evaporated milk and butter in 3-quart heavy saucepan. Cook over medium heat, stirring constantly, until mixture comes to a boil. Continue cooking to soft ball stage (234°), about 10 - 12 minutes. Remove from heat.

Blend in marshmallow crème and vanilla. Remove 2 cups of hot mixture to bowl of butterscotch pieces and nuts. Stir until smooth. Pour into greased 9" square baking pan.

Add chocolate pieces and other 1/2 cup of nuts to remaining hot mixture. Stir until chocolate is melted and mixture is smooth. Spoon evenly over butterscotch layer and spread lightly with spatula to make even layer.

Cover and refrigerate until firm. Cut into 1 1/2" squares.

Yields 35 pieces

Diana Davis

This is my Grandma's recipe; she first made it in 1978 and brought it to New England for Christmas for nearly 30 years.

Spiced Oyster Crackers

12 oz pkg oyster crackers
1/2 cup vegetable oil
1 oz envelope ranch dressing
1 tsp dry dill weed or 1 T snipped fresh dill
1/2 tsp lemon pepper

Heat the oil, combine the other ingredients and pour over the oyster crackers. Stir and serve.

Serves a bunch, in a medium size bowl.

Carol Carter

This is a recipe for spiced oyster crackers that Bessie Carter used to make for the party after the Round the Island Race.

"Better is a dinner of herbs where love is, than a stalled ox and hatred therewith."

Proverbs 15:17

Brown Sugar Frosting

1 1/3 cups white sugar
2/3 cup brown sugar
2/3 cup cream
1/2 cup butter

Cook over medium heat the above until soft ball stage. It begins at 234° on a candy thermometer.

Chill in cold/ice water until consistency for spreading. Pour over cooled cake and don't try to spread! Excellent on yellow cake (especially a package mix with eggs and butter added).

Yields enough for 1 layer.

Mayotta Kendrick

This frosting was Mayotta's specialty. Although she shared the recipe, not all achieved the same success that she did.

Chinook Salmon & Fish Sauce

1/4 cup juice from two limes
2 T Thai-type fish sauce
1 tsp minced garlic
3 T fresh mint, chopped
1/2 cup cilantro, chopped
1 tsp red chili pepper flakes
1/2 cup olive or canola oil

Combine all ingredients and shake.

Note. If you freeze some for later, don't add lime juice until ready to serve fish.

Makes about 1 cup of tasty sauce.

Gwyn Fletcher

"Strange to see how a good dinner and feasting reconcile everybody."

Summer Party Mix

2 1/2 cups corn chex type cereal
2 1/2 cups rice chex type cereal
1 1/2 cups macadamia nuts
1/3 cup butter
2 T sugar
2 T corn syrup
1 cup flaked coconut
6 oz pkg dried pineapple, chopped
1 cup white baking chips

In a large bowl, combine cereals and nuts; set aside. In a small bowl, combine the butter, sugar and corn syrup. Microwave, uncovered, for 2 minutes, stirring once or twice. Pour over cereal mixture and toss to coat.

Cook cereal mixture, microwave uncovered on high for 2 minutes, stirring once or twice. Add coconut. Cook 2 minutes longer, stirring once or twice. Spread onto waxed paper to cool. Stir in pineapple and white chips. Store in an airtight container.

Yields 3 quarts.

Cooper Wiens

This is a favorite of Cooper and his sister Stella when they visit Deer Isle from Colorado. They are grandchildren of Dick Davis.

Syb's Piccalilli

8 quarts green tomatoes, ground with food grinder
2 quarts onion, ground, chopped or grated
1/3 cup salt
1 1/2 tsp ground cinnamon
1 tsp ground cloves
1 tsp allspice
1/2 tsp ground nutmeg
1/8 tsp ground pepper
1 quart granulated sugar
2 cups white or apple cider vinegar

Prepare the onions and tomatoes and let soak with the salt overnight.

Drain and add all the rest of the ingredients. Mix all well. Cook together until tender, about 3/4 hour. Put into sterilized or dish washer clean and hot jars. Seal the jars and try to save for winter.

Yields 10 - 11 pints

Charlotte W. Davis

Syb Davis was Gwen Davis' sister-in-law and made this version with nutmeg. Hubby Frank always loves this to perk up winter meals or anytime we have fish. Gwen was my mother-in-law.

Way to Anna's Heart Pasta Sauce

16 oz can of crushed tomatoes, plain
1 1/2 lbs hot Italian sausage
1/3 cup fresh basil, chopped
Few dashes of red wine
4 cloves garlic, minced
1 large yellow onion, chopped
2 T olive oil
1 lb pasta (optional)

Heat up the olive oil in a thick-bottomed, large skillet. Add the onion and cook until translucent. Remove sausage from casings, and then add to pan. Cook thoroughly and then add the garlic. Cook a bit longer, then add the tomatoes, basil and red wine. Turn heat to low and simmer sauce until it cooks down to your desired consistency.

This is enough sauce for one pound of pasta.

Isaac Dworsky

I like to put it over thin spaghetti. Instead of Parmesan we sometimes get really good ricotta from the health food store and mix basil and a little bit of olive oil into the cheese. Yum! This is especially good if the sausage is very hot, as it cools it down perfectly.

Granola from Uncle Ed

3 cups uncooked oats, regular not instant
1 cup grape nuts
1 cup wheat or oat bran
1 cup wheat germ
1 cup flakey cereal

In bottom of greased roasting pan place all the above ingredients.

In small saucepan heat:
1/2 cup honey
1/2 cup canola or other vegetable oil
1 T molasses

Pour this over the dry ingredients in pan and mix. Bake 20 minutes at 350° oven, removing and stirring every 5 minutes.

When cool, store in an air-tight container.

Makes about 7 cups.

Eliza Childs

Cranberry Raspberry Relish

1 lb cranberries, finely chopped
2 Granny Smith apples, cored and finely chopped
1/2 - 1 cup sugar to taste
1/2 cup orange marmalade
10 oz pkg frozen raspberries, thawed and drained
1 tsp lemon juice

Mix all ingredients in large bowl. Put in a covered jar. This keeps well in the refrigerator for several weeks.

I often chop cranberries with 1/2 cup sugar in a food processor, then add to large bowl with the other ingredients, adding more sugar if needed.

Kellie Coombs

This is a family favorite. We especially enjoy using Nervous Nellie's Sunshine Road marmalade in the recipe. Besides Thanksgiving when I first started making this, it is nice with a pork roast, ham or with any turkey or ham in a sandwich.

Fruit Salsa Tropicale

4 cups diced fresh tropical fruit of your choice such as mango, papaya, pineapple
1 medium red onion, chopped fine
1/2 cup cilantro, chopped fine
2 fresh limes, juiced
3 cloves garlic, minced
1 or 2 red chili peppers, seeded and minced
3 T of your best olive oil
1 T white vinegar (I prefer rice wine vinegar)
Pinches of pepper and kosher salt to taste
Dash of cayenne to taste

Combine all ingredients and refrigerate. This is an excellent sauce for grilled fish.

Makes about 5 cups, and may be stored in the fridge for a few days.

Lynne Wiley

"All you need is love. But a little chocolate now and then doesn't hurt."

Charles M Schutz

The Perfect Anthem

5 basses
5 tenors
4 altos
6 sopranos

Lay basses flat in the pew and pound with a mallet until soft. Spread with butter and place in a slow oven to toast the tone.

Finely chop tenors, add 3 T allspice and a cup of lemon juice to cut the high notes and bring out the color. Allow to rest.

Melt altos in a heavy saucepan, stirring constantly to a smooth, rich sound.

Drop sopranos into a mixer, one by one, beating well after each addition, until they stand in soft peaks.

Remove basses from oven. Spread altos evenly over them, blending carefully at edges.

Sprinkle tenors over the entire dish and top with dollops of sopranos.

Return the dish to the choir pews, bake for 30 minutes and serve to waiting parishioners.

Serves an entire congregation.

Win Pusey

Sunset Anniversary Scripture Cake

1 cup Jeremiah 6:20
1 T Judges 5:25
2 Isaiah 10:14
1 cup Judges 4:19
1 tsp Amos 4:5
2 cup 1 Kings 4:22
1/2 tsp Leviticus 2:13
1 cup 1 Samuel 30:11
Season to taste 1 Kings 10:10
According to 2 Chronicles 9:9

Preheat oven to 375°.

Cream Jeremiah 6:20 and Judges 5:25 together.

Add unbeaten Isaiah 10:14, one at a time and mix well.

Add Amos 4:5 to Judges 4:19 and stir until it foams. Then add to above mixture. Sift 1 Kings 4:22 with Mark 9:50 and 1 tsp 1 Kings 10:10 after taking some of the Kings 4:22 to mix with 1 Samuel 30:11.

Add the dry ingredients to the wet batter and mix to combine. Stir in 1 Samuel 30:11.

Scrape into greased loaf pan or 9" x 3" plain tube pan. Bake for about 35 to 40 minutes. Cool 5 minutes and remove from pan to rack to finish cooling.

This serves 8-10 of those who ponder God's word.

Follow Solomon's prescription for eating cake. Proverbs 14:23.

And always remember Matthew 6:25-26.

Charlo Davis

Popovers

2 eggs
1 cup milk
1 cup sifted all-purpose flour
1/2 tsp salt

Grease popover tins well with nonstick spray. Break eggs into a bowl. Add remaining ingredients and mix well with a spoon or a fork. Disregard lumps.

Fill tins 3/4 full. Put into a cold oven. Set oven at 450º. Bake 28 minutes. Do not open door during baking.

Recipe can be doubled, keeping salt to 1/2 tsp.

After 28 minutes, turn oven off. Crack oven door open slightly so popovers will cool slowly. Remove and let stand a few minutes and remove from tin.

Serve with butter and honey.

Yields 4 popovers

Janet Rice

Seashore Shirred Sunshine Eggs

1 T butter or oil
1/4 cup chopped onions
3 thin slices of smoked salmon
5 capers
1 T chopped dill
Whole egg
Dill sprigs for garnish

Preheat oven to 350º.

Add butter or oil to each dish and heat dish in oven. Add chopped onion, stir to coat, and bake until almost brown. Remove from oven. Add capers and chopped dill. Add salmon slices. Break egg on top. Put back in oven. Bake until egg is set, basting, if you like. Serve with sprig of fresh dill.

Serves 1

Ginger Reiman

I made up this recipe that I served to house guests and to my weekly walking group at the end of our walk.

"While the pot boils, friendships endure."

Beach Hill Relish

1 peck green tomatoes (8 quarts)
2 quarts onions, chopped
1/3 cup horseradish, grated fresh or prepared
1 1/2 tsp ground cloves
2 tsp ground cinnamon
2 tsp allspice
2 tsp mustard
6 cups granulated sugar
2 cups vinegar, or more
1/2 cup salt

Wash the tomatoes and chop or put them through a meat grinder. Let stand overnight with the salt.

When ready, drain and add all the other ingredients in a canner. Stir to combine well.

Cook together until tender, which amounts to boiling for about 3/4 hour. Put into sterilized jars and seal.

Makes about 10 pints.

Gwendolyn Greenlaw Davis

I always gathered and ground my horseradish and shared enough of it with all of my daughters-in-law so that they could make their own. This was my grandmother Clara Howard's recipe.

Hard Sauces

Almond or Vanilla Hard Sauce
1/2 cup butter
1/2 cup powdered sugar or white granulated sugar
1 T brandy
2 drops vanilla or almond extract

Orange Hard Sauce
3/4 cup butter
1 1/2 cups powdered sugar
2 T brandy or Grand Marnier
1 tsp grated orange peel or 1/2 tsp orange extract

For either recipe, cream butter and sugar together. (If using white sugar, cream until it is not grainy.) Combine with rest of ingredients. Cover and chill until ready to serve.

Bring butter spread to room temperature before serving. It should be the consistency of butter. Can put a dollop on when serving and pass the rest around. Or, you can make it pretty, or not, and just pass it around.

Serves 6 - 10

Charlotte W. Davis

Hard sauce is rich and sweet. It is great with warmed mincemeat pies, mincemeat squares, plum pudding, fruitcake, gingerbread and pumpkin desserts.

A small sprig of holly with red berries makes a very festive presentation.

It is easier to cream with a hand mixer, but I have fond memories of my sister-in-law, who shares my name, and I, stirring this lovingly by hand, in anticipation of having it with Gwen's holiday steamed pudding.

Animal Treats

Dog Treats:
1 cup all-purpose flour
1 cup wheat flour
1/2 cup wheat germ
1/2 cup non-fat dry milk
6 T margarine or butter
1 egg
1 T brown sugar
3 T liver powder or veggie flakes
1/2 cup water

Preheat oven to 325°. Combine all ingredients; the mixture will be stiff. Roll it out to about 1/4" thick and cut with bone shaped cookie cutter. Bake for 30 minutes.

Yields 3 dozen

Cat Treats:
1 1/2 cups rolled oats, ground
1/4 cup vegetable oil or 1 egg
1/2 cup flour
12 oz can salmon or chicken with liquid

Preheat oven to 350°. Mix all ingredients. Flour your hands and make pinches of the dough into small, 1/2" thick round treats. Set on greased cookie sheet and bake for 30 minutes or until treats are slightly browned. Cool carefully before serving.

Makes 3 dozen.

Anette Jaquette

We include these in honor of the sweet canines, felines and other animals that come for the Blessing of the Animals in the Sunset Village Green garden by our church each year.

"Doggie" Birthday Cake
Peanut Butter Carrot Cake

1 cup flour (use buckwheat or rice flour to avoid wheat sensitivities)
1 tsp baking soda
1/4 cup peanut butter
1/4 cup vegetable oil
1 cup shredded carrots
1 tsp vanilla
1/3 cup honey
1 egg

Optional:
Cottage cheese or cream cheese icing of your choice
Carrots or dog treats

Mix flour and baking soda. Add remaining ingredients.

Pour into 8" round cake pan and bake at 350 degrees for 30 minutes. Let cool.

For icing, you can puree cottage cheese in blender or use cream cheese. Decorate with carrots or dog treats.

Makes one 8" round cake.

Mariner and Zoom Simmons

Portuguese Water Dogs of Lois and Carl Simmons

William Harris and Norm Dunbar

Rev. Owen Speaker, Eliza and Chris Childs

New Trad Trio

CHAPTER 13

Ecclesiastes 8:15

And I commend joy, for man has no good thing under the sun but to eat and drink and be joyful, for this will go with him in his toil through the days of his life that God has given him under the sun.

Island Wedding Reception Menu For 50 Guests

My youngest son and his fiancée decided that they would like to have their wedding ceremony on a beach. That beach ended up being in front of our house! They wanted the day to be casual with a picnic theme. We had red and white checked tablecloths, hydrangea flower arrangements for the tables, white and red balsam sachets tied with red and white checked ribbons, small votives in glass jars with periwinkle shells, and sea glass and various shells scattered on the tables. The New Trad Trio from Blue Hill provided some enjoyable music. And, amazingly for the coast of Maine, the weather was picture perfect!

Suzanne Decrow

MENU

Appetizers

Parsley Herb Dip with Crudités
Mussels Marinara
Crabmeat and Lemon Ricotta Vol Au Vents
Assorted Olives
Sliced Watermelon

Dinner

Individual Seafood Frittatas
BBQ Chicken
Root Beer Baked Beans
Toasted Israeli Couscous with Vegetables and Lemon Balsamic Vinaigrette
Grammie Cel's Potato Salad
Mixed Greens with Blueberry Vinaigrette
Cuban Bread: This recipe for Cuban bread may be found in the Breads & Rolls section.

Blueberry Vinaigrette

1/2 cup olive oil
1/4 cup balsamic vinegar
1 clove garlic, chopped
1 T green pepper, chopped
1 T onion, chopped
1 tsp sugar
1 cup frozen or fresh blueberries

Place all the ingredients in a food processor and blend until puréed. Refrigerate.

Yields 1 1/2 cups

I doubled this recipe to serve 50 with plenty of mixed greens for it to cover.

Suzanne Decrow

"If you judge people, you have no time to love them."

Mother Teresa

Mussels Marinara

5 lbs mussels
Cold water to cover
8 oz salsa (temperature of your choice)
1/4 cup butter
3 T olive oil
1/2 cup red onion, minced
4 garlic cloves, minced
1 tsp fresh rosemary, chopped
1 tsp dried oregano
1 T fresh parsley, chopped
1 cup dry white wine, or more

Place mussels in a large kettle and cover with cold water. Inspect each mussel and discard any that do not close when tapped gently with a knife. Scrub each one, scrape off any barnacles with a knife, and de-beard.

In another large cooking pot, combine the remaining ingredients and simmer for 30 seconds. Add the mussels and more wine, if desired, and continue simmering until all the shells are opened.

I tripled the recipe to serve 50 as appetizers and served them in my large glass bowl.

Suzanne Decrow

Parsley Herb Dip with Crudités

1 clove garlic
1/2 tsp salt
1 cup packed fresh parsley
1 scallion cut into 1" pieces
1 cup mayonnaise
1/2 cup sour cream
1 tsp chopped fresh thyme
1/4 tsp freshly ground pepper

Place garlic and salt in a food processor and process until the garlic is minced. Add the parsley and scallion and process until finely chopped. Add the mayonnaise, sour cream, thyme and pepper and process until well mixed. Cover and chill.

Yields 2 cups

I doubled the recipe and served it with a variety of fresh vegetables.

Suzanne Decrow

Individual Seafood Frittatas

3 medium yellow squash
2 red bell peppers
1 yellow bell pepper
1 medium red onion, peeled
2 garlic cloves, minced
3 T olive oil
6 large eggs
1/4 cup whipping cream
3 T chopped fresh basil
1 1/2 tsp kosher salt
1 tsp saffron threads
1/2 tsp freshly ground pepper
1 pound combined fresh seafood: lobster, scallops, shrimp, crabmeat, etc.
2 5 oz pkgs of garlic-herb cheese spread
8 oz shredded Swiss cheese
Parsley for garnish

Cut squash into 1/4" thick slices. Cut bell peppers into 1/4" strips. Cut onion in half lengthwise and cut in slices.

In a large skillet, sauté the squash, bell peppers, onion and garlic in the olive oil for 5-10 minutes or until crisp tender.

In a large bowl, whisk together the eggs, cream, basil, salt, saffron and pepper.

Stir in the seafood, cheeses and sautéed vegetables. Divide mixture in well-buttered cup cake pans.

Bake at 350° for about 20 minutes. Let sit for 10 minutes before removing from pans. Can be made a day ahead and refrigerated.

Reheat before serving and garnish with parsley.

Yields 5 dozen frittatas

Suzanne Decrow

Lemon Ricotta Vol Au Vents

1 lb ricotta cheese
2 T lemon zest
3 T fresh basil, chopped or 1 T dry
Salt and pepper to taste
2 boxes 15-count mini phyllo shells (a.k.a. fillo)
Honey to drizzle

Combine the first three ingredients and chill to combine the flavors. Remove from refrigerator and adjust seasonings. Spoon flavored ricotta mixture into the shells, on a tray or platter, just before serving.

Drizzle each shell lightly with honey.

Yields 30 shells

Suzanne Decrow

Crabmeat Vol Au Vents

2 lbs of fresh crabmeat
Mayonnaise, enough to lightly coat the crabmeat
1/4 cup chopped chives
Salt and pepper to taste
3 boxes 15-count mini phyllo (a.k.a. fillo, filo) shells
Chopped chives to garnish

Gently combine the crabmeat with the mayonnaise and chives. Spoon mixture into shells just before serving.

Garnish with a few chopped chives.

Yields 42 to 45 shells

Suzanne Decrow

"My tastes are simple; I am satisfied with the best."

Winston S. Churchill

Root Beer Baked Beans

4 slices apple wood-smoked bacon, cut into 1" pieces
3 1/2 cups chopped onions
2 garlic cloves, minced
4 15 oz cans of cannelloni beans, drained
1 1/2 cups root beer
3 T apple cider vinegar
3 T light molasses
2 T tomato paste
2 T Dijon mustard
1 1/2 tsp chili powder
1 tsp kosher salt
1 tsp freshly ground pepper

Cook bacon in a large ovenproof pot over medium heat until crisp, stirring occasionally. Using a slotted spoon, transfer to paper towels to drain. Add the onions to the drippings in the pot and brown, stirring often, for about 8 minutes. Add the garlic and stir for one minute. Add the beans, root beer, vinegar, molasses, tomato paste, mustard, chili powder, salt and pepper and mix well. Stir in the bacon and bring to a boil.

Transfer to the oven and bake uncovered at 400º until the liquid thickens, about 40 minutes.

Serves 16

Suzanne Decrow

Israeli Couscous & Roasted Vegetables

2 cups Israeli couscous, "big like pearls"
12 spears asparagus, cut into 1" pieces
2 medium zucchini, halved and cut into 1" pieces
2 small yellow squash, halved and cut into 1" pieces
1/2 cup kalamata olives, pitted and halved
Olive oil to drizzle
2 T fresh basil leaves, chopped or 1+ T dried basil
Freshly ground black pepper, to taste
1 T salt
2 large red peppers, sliced and cut into 1" pieces

In a large skillet over high heat, toast the couscous until golden. Bring 6 cups of water to a boil, add the salt and toasted couscous, and cook for 8 - 9 minutes. Drain well and let cool. Put the asparagus, squashes and peppers in a large roasting pan and drizzle with olive oil to coat. Roast in the oven at 400º for about 30 - 45 minutes until beginning to brown.

In a large bowl, combine the couscous, roasted vegetables, olives and basil. Season with pepper to taste.

Prepare the Lemon Balsamic Vinaigrette:

1 small shallot, minced
3 T fresh lemon juice
1 tsp lemon zest
3 T aged balsamic vinegar
1 T red wine vinegar
Salt and freshly ground pepper
3/4 cup extra virgin olive oil

Combine the first 6 ingredients in a small bowl and then whisk in the oil. Pour over the couscous and vegetable mixture and combine well.

This is a great summer salad. I sometimes add sundried tomatoes and capers to the salad.

Serves 16

Suzanne Decrow

Mayotta's Classic Lobster Picnic

Mayotta Kendrick's Lobster Picnic Must-Haves:

Bug spray
Large wash tub with lid
Firewood, paper, matches
Cinder blocks for making beach fireplace
Ice
Plastic glasses
Mixes, including lemonade
Assorted liquor
Beer
White wine
Lemons, limes
Knife
Crackers and cheese
Chips, nuts, popcorn

For the Main Course:

Lobsters, forks, picks
One lb butter per each 16 people
Butter cups
Plates, napkins, paper towels
Salads, small plates and forks
Serving fork and spoon
Lettuce sandwiches
For Dessert:
Cake, knife, small plates, pies, brownies or fruit
Coffee, pot, milk, sugar, cups and spoons

To cook the lobsters, bring about 3" of salt water to the boil. Remove the rubber bands from the lobsters, and drop them in head first, and allow to come to the boil again. From this second boil, time about 16 minutes more. (Andy says lobsters are ready when he has finished his second beer!) Another way to test for doneness is if the lobster falls away from an antenna when dangled. Visitors may want their cameras when the steaming orange lobsters are dumped on the beach.

Chris Ramsdale

For An Island Beach Picnic

Mayotta Kendrick's (1922-2010) Island Picnic Must-Haves

You need to bring the following:

Grills and grate
Spatula
Fork
Pot holders
Knife for butter
Paper
Matches
Paper towels (napkins)
Paper plates
Plastic glasses
Utensils
Hot dogs
Hamburgers
Rolls for hot dogs and hamburgers
Butter
Mustard
Relish
Ketchup
Onion
Mayo
Tomatoes
Lettuce
Chips
Desserts--fruit, brownies, cookies
Lemonade, beer, soft drinks, water, cooler for soft drinks and perishables
Ice
Plastic bags for trash and recyclables

Just add a nice sunny summer day, family and friends!

Dear friend of Mayotta's found these lists at the Salmon Point cottage.

Ina Pavlova-Ramsdale

THE COOKIES
Barbara L.H. Chesney, Charlo Davis, Carol Bischoff, Anette Jaquette, Lanny Anderson, Del Rosenfield

Eliza Spencer, the last Cookie emerges from hiding.

Silken Tassels

Vibrant green sentinels rustling row upon row
Clutching the contoured, furrowed dark earth below
Flowing tassels waving their silken tipped crowns
Evident bucolic abundance so richly abounds.

Summer's glad harvest beckons, the gathering begins
Amidst sun-drenched days, the soft caressing winds
Earlier vigor, toils, aspirations when planted
The season runs strong, Spring's rich promise is granted.

`Tis the time of the harvest, the cherished reward it draws nigh
Green waves reach heavenward, impaling the sky
To farm stands and markets, throughout the broad stretch of land
Sheaths of bright green, showcasing silken essence so grand.

Soon breads and soufflés and savory hot ears
Enhance kitchens and tables as in former years
Relishes, fritters, succotash, puddings and soup
From this magnificent offering of the agrarian group.

Fresh bounty from the fields, farm to market to table
Magnify this grand season, as long as we are able
We forget not the bounty, amidst life's pace so swift,
Voices raised to the Perfecter, for life's abundant gifts.

Tim Vander Mel of Deer Isle, ME and Vero Beach, FL

List of References for History of Sunset Congregational Church

1. Local history from residents of Deer Isle.

2. Frey, Hugh B. Two Centuries, The History of the First Congregational Church of Deer Isle, Maine, 1773-1973. Rockland, Maine: Maine Coast Printers, 1973.

3. Deer Isle Comprehensive Plan Update: Inventory and Analysis. Deer Isle Comprehensive Planning Committee, 2006.

4. Chronology provided by an unknown person and added to by Ruth and Bob Harris and Susan Harris Seater. Deer Isle, Maine: Deer Isle-Stonington Historical Society.

5. "Bits of Local History." Blue Hill, Maine: The Weekly Packet, 1975.

6. Hosmer, Frances L. "Early History of the Martha Washington Benevolent Society," written at the age of 92 years old for their Centennial. Stonington, Maine, 1935.

7. "The Sunset Congregational Church." Notes. Deer Isle, Maine: Deer Isle-Stonington Historical Society.

8. MWBS Notes v.1896-1919. Deer Isle, Maine: Deer Isle-Stonington Historical Society.

9. Organizational Chart of the Sunset Congregational Church. Deer Isle, Maine.

Sunset Church Grace

To the Tune of the Doxology:

Be present at our table Lord
Be here and everywhere adored
These mercies bless and grant that we
May feast in Paradise with Thee.

Amen

INDEX of RECIPES

SALADS

Autumn Island Salad……………………………… 19
Broccoli Peanut Salad……………………………..25
Broccoli Slaw……………………………………….22
Brook Cove Bean Salad……………………………20
Cabbage Crunch Salad…………………………….16
Carottes Aux Chalets Français……………………..24
Chinese Chicken Salad……………………………..32
Cranberry Spinach Feta Salad……………………..22
Curried Brown Rice Salad………………………….20
Downeast Mandarin Orange Salad………………..25
Early Spring Cheese Salad…………………………26
Easy Corn Pea Salad……………………………….23
Eggemoggin Tofu Salad……………………………21
Family Cabbage Waldorf Salad……………………26
German Salad……………………………………… 27
Green Dream Salad………………………………...21
Green Veggie & Fruit Salad……………………….. 27
Harbor Eggplant Salad……………………………..28
Heidi's Green Bean Salad…………………………..28
Island Chicken Salad……………………………….18
Israeli Couscous & Roasted Vegetables……… …..212
Jazzy Black Bean Salad ……………………………17
Karen's Broccoli Salad………………………………19
Lobster & Wild Rice Salad……………….. ……..24
Marilyn's Broccoli Salad…………………………...29
Musketeers Frozen Slaw……………………………29
Northeast Cabbage Salad………………………......23
Orange Pineapple Salad…………………………… 18
Sunset Chicken Summer Salad……………………17
Periwinkle Orange-pineapple Salad……………….16
Sauerkraut Salad……………………………………30
Ship Ahoy Summer Salad………………………….30
Southeast Hills Cider Salad………………………..31
Spaghetti Salad……………………………………..31
Tasty Tabouleh & Parsley Salad……………………32

APPETIZERS

Artichoke Dip……………………………………….37
Cheesy Chanterelle Mushroom Bake……………..39
Cheese Puff Canapés……………………………….38
Cheese Spread………………………………………39
Chutney Cheese Canapé……………………………40
Curry Paté……………………………………….. ..41
Deviled & Angel Eggs……………………………..42
Dijon Mustard Green Onion……………………… 42
Easy Spinach Dip……………………………….. ..43
Flank Steak Appetizer……………………….. ……37
Gorgonzola Walnut Rounds……………….............43
Horseradish Dip……………………………………44
Hot Cheese Crackers ……………………………...44
Hot Pizza Dip………………………………………40
Island Crap Dip……………………………………41
Mini Blts……………………………………………45
Mom's Crabmeat Dip……………………………..47
Olive and Nut Cheese Ball………………………..47
Pesto Dip…………………………………………..45
Port Wine Cheese Ball……………………………..38
Shore & Hen-house Quiche……………………….46
Shrimp Ball……………………………………......48
Smoked Salmon Bites……………………………..48
Summer Party Mix……………………………….198
Spiced Oyster Crackers ………………………….196
Vegetarian, Gluten-free Yummies……………......46

SOUPS

Black Bean Soup with Garnishes…………………53
Broccoli, Bean & Cheddar Soup………………….55
Celebration Fork & Spoon Soup………………….54
Chilled Cranberry Soup…………………. ………52
Clamdigger Navy Bean Soup……………………..52
Cold Cucumber Soup……………………………..54
Cold Peach Soup in White Wine………………….53
Curried Pumpkin Bisque………………………….56
Italian Sausage Soup………………………….…..55
Yukon Gold Potato and Leek Soup……..………. ...56

BEVERAGES

Ash Lane Rhubarb Punch………………………....62
Blueberry Shrub…………………………………...63
Counterbalance …………………………………...63
Earl Grey-type Herbed Ice Tea…………………...64
Healthful Green Smoothie…………………….. ...60
Hot Orange Tea…………………………………...60
Judge Claybough's Eggnog……………………….64
Melon Cooler ……………………………………..65
Pomegranny ………………………………………61
Red Raspberry Limeade…………………………..65
Rhubarb Juice……………………………………..66
Strawberry-Banana Smoothie……………………..61
Sweet Ginger Tisane………………………………62
Village Green Punch………………………………66

BREADS & ROLLS

All Bran Refrigerator Rolls......................70
Apricot Bread...70
Banana Bread..74
Beer Batter Bread....................................71
Bran Muffins..78
Cardamom Raisin Bread.........................75
Christmas Bread......................................71
Corn Meal Griddle Cakes........................74
Cottage Cheese Dill Bread......................75
Cuban Bread..76
Grandmother's Irish Soda Bread..............76
New England Raisin Bread......................77
Norwegian Cracked Wheat Bread............72
Popovers..202
Poppy Seed Bread...................................72
Rolled Oats Yeast Bread..........................77
Whole Wheat Pizza Dough – Double......78
Whole Wheat Quick Bread......................73
Yorkshire Pudding 73

COOKIES AND BARS

Almond Cookies......................................82
Bessie Gray's Shed Sugar Cookes...........83
Butterscotch Bars....................................83
Chewy Maple Cookies.............................82
Comfort Cookies.....................................85
Cookie Dough Brownies.........................86
Deerfield Sugar and Spice Cookies.........87
Diana's Spice Runner Cookies................84
Fruit-oatmeal Bars...................................91
Ginger Crunch Cookies...........................88
Granola Bars...88
Gwen's Brambles....................................86
Judy Friend's Hermits.............................89
Kyra's Lemon Squares............................85
Mama's Good Cookies............................89
Mar's Lemon Squares.............................92
Mincemeat Squares.................................93
Molasses Crinkles...................................87
Nancy's Lace Cookies.............................90
No Bake Chocolate Peanut Butter Bars...90
Orange Chocolate Chip Cookies.............91
Parisian Sweets.......................................84
Pumpkin Chocolate Chip Cookies..........94
Ruby's Split-second Shortbread..............94
Saucy Bars..93
Simple Cookies.......................................92

DESSERTS

Allie's Mincemeat Pie............................. 98
Angel Pie.. .99
Arlene's Pie Crust & Ottsie's Pie............118
Bell Buoy Fruit Torte............................. 113
Bible Study Carrot Cake........................ 119
Billy's Coconut Cake & Frosting...................120
Black Midnight Cake.............................. 99
Blueberry Dessert with Pineapple..........119
Boiled Raisin Fruit Cake........................100
Bon Temps New Orleans Bread Pudding..........100
Buoy Blueberry Cake.............................108
Burnt Cove Blueberry Cake....................122
Cherry Cream Cheese Pie......................101
Chocolate Coffee Rum Cake..................101
Chocolate Erotica...................................105
Chocolate Macadamia Nut Torte............120
Coffee Angel Food Cake........................122
Cold Lemon Soufflé...............................102
Cracker Pie and Strawberries.................102
Cranberry Pies..116
Creme Puffs a la Brittney 114
Cutter Key Lime Pie...............................108
Danish Ris A' La Manda Dessert...........103
Deer Isle Grapenut Pudding...................116
Dump-it-all-in Cake................................121
Eagle Island Easy Fruit Torte.................118
Fresh Maine Blueberry Pie.....................105
Frozen Yogurt Pie for Marthas...............106
Fruit Cake a La Alice and Allen.............107
Gluten-free Bûche De Noël....................117
Grandmother's Old English Plum Pudding.........107
Island Miracle Cake...............................103
Joy's Easy Chocolate Mousse Pie..........104
Lily Pond Chocolate Pudding.................104
Maine Blueberry Cake............................109
Mrs. Washburn's Pineapple Pudng.........124
Mrs. Wood's Pound Cake.......................109
Old-fashioned Carrot Cake.....................124
Peachy Pie..126
Pecan Caramel Custard...........................123
Pots De Crème.......................................110
Pumpkin Pudding...................................110
Raspberry Walnut Torte.........................111
Rhubarb Cake...111
Rhubarb Crisp..113
Rum Cake...112
Shaker Floating Island...........................121
Simple Elegance for Chocoholics..........125
Suffield Fruit Berry Cobbler..................126

Delicious Deer Isle

Summer Berry Sorbet..123
Susan and Elizabeth's Gingerbread......................114
Susie Wakelin's Lemon Chiffon...........................115
Swedish Almond Cake.. 98
Sylvester's Spiced Peaches...................................106
Tiramisu sans Oeuf...115
Warm Rice Pudding"Julegrød"..........................125
Zucchini Pineapple Cake......................................112

MAIN DISHES

All Day Beef Stew..131
Bacon, Macaroni & Cheese Casserole..............142
Beef Taiwan...142
Beef and Black Bean Chili...................................147
Breast of Chicken in Cream Sauce.....................130
Causeway White Chili..141
Charlo's Party Lasagna.......................................132
Chicken Divan with Rice.....................................144
Chicken and Lentil Stew......................................144
Chicken & Apples..143
Chicken Cacciatore...143
Chicken Marbella...133
Chicken Joy..145
Chicken with Spiced Cherries.............................138
Country Style Spare Ribs....................................145
Crabmeat Vol Au Vents.......................................211
Deer Isle Dal..146
Drunken Meat Balls...139
Easy Lamb Stew..133
Family Meat Loaf-crockpot.................................134
Frikkedeller (Danish Meatballs).........................135
Garbure...146
Giuliano's Moroccan Chicken.............................137
Little Deer Isle Roast Lamb................................140
Meghan's Pesto Chicken......................................131
My Mother's Ham Loaf.......................................135
Oceanville Beef Stew...130
Pasta E Fagioli..136
Pentecostal Penne..141
Pete Chesney's Rare Rib Roast...........................138
Prosciutto, Asparagus and Mushrooms.............134
Really Good Pumpkin Stew a La Shirley..........132
Spanakopita (Greek Spinach Pie)......................147
Spicy Scallop and Cauliflower Stew...................176
Steven's Sweet and Sour Shrimp........................166
Stuffed Pasta Shells...136
Swedish Meatballs...140
Vegetable Casserole...152
Winona Chang's Honey Lemon Chicken...........139
Wonderful Meatloaf with Sauce..........................137

VEGETABLES AND SIDE DISHES

A B Cup Vegetable Casserole..........................154
Basil Pesto, Squashed Tomatoes....................155
Broccoli with Orange Sauce............................150
Cheesy Potatoes..155
Clapshot..158
Corn Souffle Casserole....................................151
Courgettes Farcies Provencales......................158
Creamed Corn a La Donnis............................151
Danish Red Cabbage 153
German Red Cabbage.......................................159
Gram's Baked Beans..156
Grazia's Asparagus Pesto................................156
Krispy Kale...150
Nancy Torrey's Cheese Squash.......................157
Pumpkin Island Pumpkin................................159
Rodbedesallad (Beet Salad)............................160
Root Beer Baked Beans....................................212
Sister Mary's Zesty Carrots.............................152
String Beans with an Indian Accent................161
Stuffed Baked Potatoes....................................160
Sunshine Summer Squash...............................153
Tina's Baked Beans..157
Vegetable Casserole...152
Yam Casserole..161
Zucchini "Cakes"..154

SEAFOOD

Baked Stuffed Haddock....................................164
Christmas Eve Red & White Stew..................171
Cod with Miso Glaze..176
Coveside Crab Melt..171
Crab Cheese Puff..165
Crabby Crab Cakes..162
Dick Bridges' Lobster Chowder......................170
How to Prepare and Freeze Lobster...............177
Howard Corning's Mill Island Crab Whiffle...166
Individual Seafood Frittatas 210
Island Summer Cod...172
Jackie Dunbar's Baked Haddock....................165
Lobster and Leek Pasta...................................172
Macaroni & Brie with Crab.............................173
Maine Fish Chowder..168
Maple Balsamic Salmon for Two....................173
Marshall Island Scallop Chowdah..................170
Mussel Chowder with Veggies........................174
Mussels Marinara...209
Peekytoe Crabmeat Rolls.................................174
Penobscot Chowder..169

Pressy Village Pesto Pasta..........................175
Ray's Crab Cakes...167
Roast Shrimp Plus..168
Sand Beach Ginger Mussels........................167
Scallop Cheese Puff.....................................175
Sicilian Fish Soup...169
Spicy Scallop and Cauliflower Stew............176
Steven's Sweet and Sour Shrimp.................166

BREAKFASTS AND BRUNCH

Blue Lemon Poppy Coffee Cake..................180
Caramel-soaked French Toast.....................186
Cardamom Coffee Cake..............................180
Christmas Brunch Casserole.......................181
Coffee Cake...181
Ginger Raisin Scones..................................182
Goat Cheese & Herb Frittata.......................182
Green Tomato Breakfast Cake....................183
Lowe's Road Breakfast Apple Cake............183
Maggie Spofford's Crabmeat Quiche..........185
Oeufs En Cocottes à La Polly.....................185
Southern (Risen) Buckwheat Cakes............184
The Pancake...184
Versatile Griddle Cakes..............................186

THIS AND THAT

5 Minute Chocolate Mug Cake....................190
Animal Treats..204
Beach Hill Relish...203
Blueberry Vinaigrette..................................209
Bordeaux Relish..191
Brown Sugar Frosting.................................197
Chinook Salmon & Fish Sauce...................197
Claudia's Fudge..195
Cranberry Raspberry Relish.......................200
Cranberry Orange Piquant.........................195
Doggie Birthday Cake.................................204
Ellen's Fruit Dip..192
Fruit Salsa Tropicale...................................200
Granola from Uncle Ed...............................199
Hard Sauces..203
Horseradish & Mustard Sauce...................192
Marinade for Chicken.................................194
Mitli Chili Lime Peanuts.............................190
Mother's Watermelon Pickle......................194
Osprey Point Nutty Granola Bars..............191
Parsley Herb Dip with Crudité...................210
Popovers...202

Seashore Shirred Sunshine Eggs................202
Spiced Oyster Crackers..............................196
Summer Party Mix......................................198
Sunset Anniversary Scripture Cake............201
Syb's Piccalilli...198
The Perfect Anthem....................................201
Two-tone Fudge 196
Very Best Pie Pastry 193
Way to Anna's Heart Pasta Sauce 199
Zucchini Pepper Relish 193

CELEBRATIONS

For an Island Beach Picnic.........................214
Island Wedding Reception Menu for 50 Guests.....208
    Blueberry Vinaigrette............................209
    Mussels Marinara..................................209
    Parsley Herb Dip with Crudites 210
    Individual Seafood Frittatas 210
    Lemon Ricotta Vol Au Vents 211
    Crabmeat Vol Au Vents 211
    Root Beer Baked Beans 212
    Israeli Couscous & Roasted Vegetables 212
Mayotta's Classic Lobster Picnic................213